HEAVEN BOUND AMID PANDEMICS

Ken Rolheiser

The Road All Runners Come

Preface

Covid-19 has given us a chance to refocus our spiritual lives. We can choose to leave the weary soul sickness of life without hope and to focus on the Resurrection and God's promise of abundant life.

The need for this book is something I have realized over the years as a lay minister to the suffering, the dying and the grieving. Whether leading funeral prayers or visiting the sick and the dying, I shared my thoughts with them, and they found consolation. I realized though that I could more specifically address their needs in the work that follows. Toward that end I spent time listening to speakers and gathering and organizing materials.

There is a tremendous gracefulness required to die well. This is something we rarely speak about. *Dynamic Christian* says, "The Church needs a world-class program to help us deal with all these very practical issues surrounding our departure from this life."

Go to a large mirror. Check every side of you, top to bottom. Look for the *expiry date*. Sometimes it is on the lid, or on the bottom. This is not to be confused with our *best before* date. All of us have an expiry date.

When I look at life's journey, I am reminded of the Irishman who was asked for directions to Dublin. "I wouldn't start out from here," he cautioned. RIGHT NOW we are all on the road all runners come. We start from here. We are heaven bound.

Our lives are a book, and the last chapter is the key. If we could read that chapter first, it would give everything a perspective, especially our attitude toward suffering and pain, and our natural fear of death. If we live a life filled with love and gratitude, even the last part of our journey home is one we can joyfully make in faith and hope. As Christians it is possible for us to have a piece of heaven with us throughout our lives.

Introduction

Covid-19 has brought a huge boost of faith for many. Nearly three in ten U.S. adults have said that the pandemic has strengthened their faith, and four in ten say that it has strengthened family bonds.

This book addresses timely topics all of us encounter as we approach life's end - Grieving, Suicide, Palliative Care versus Euthanasia, Fear of Death, Proof of Heaven, Angels, Miracles, and Joy and Hope versus Pain and Suffering. As well, **Heaven Bound Amid Pandemics** outlines how to live a life of Love and Gratitude.

If we live our lives against an infinite horizon, we are aware of our Creator, our destiny, and hopefully, our purpose. A new shadow is dogging us in 2021, and that is Covid-19. This pandemic is creating fear and panic as well as challenges for growth. Coronavirus has triggered suicides and fear of dying alone in isolation. The guilt and difficulty of grieving where traditional funerals are not possible make these painful times. Suicide hotline calls are up 300 per cent in the United States. But there is a spiritual upside. Fear of death has led to a spiritual renaissance, and even some agnostics now contemplate hope in an immortal soul beyond this material world.

It is possible to keep our eternal goal in mind as this pandemic gives us a new focus on spirituality. God wants us to live well, but he also wants us to die well. **Heaven Bound Amid Pandemics** lights up life's journey and deals with some very practical aspects of our departure from this world.

Heaven Bound Amid Pandemics is about the joy we may anticipate at the end of the fruitful journey of our lives. Everyone comes to the end of that journey. Few are eager for it – the Saints, perhaps. Fewer still make light of it.

Oscar Wilde reflected this wit from his deathbed: "My wallpaper and I are fighting a duel to the death. One or the other of us has to go."

Some last words are optimistic. Legend has it that Beethoven declared, "I shall hear in heaven!"

Steve Jobs, co-founder of Apple Computers who died of pancreatic cancer at age 56, leaves us an inspiring legacy about death. In his eulogy his sister Mona Simpson describes his passing as embarking on a steep climb. His breath indicated this. One final time Jobs looked at his family and Laurene, his partner for life, and then looking over their shoulders he spoke his final words: "Oh wow, oh wow, oh wow."

In an earlier message Jobs quoted an essay from an author unknown which said:

> I reached the pinnacle of success in the business world. In others' eyes, my life is an epitome of success.
>
> However, aside from work, I have little joy. In the end, wealth is only a fact of life that I am accustomed to.
>
> At this moment, lying on the sick bed and recalling my whole life, I realize that all the recognition and wealth that I took so much pride in, have paled and become meaningless in the face of impending death.
>
> In the darkness, I look at the green lights from the life supporting machines and hear the humming mechanical sounds. I can feel the breath of the god of death drawing closer ….
>
> Now I know, when we have accumulated sufficient wealth to last our lifetime, we should pursue other matters that are unrelated to wealth ….
>
> [There] Should be something that is more important: perhaps relationships, perhaps art, perhaps a dream from younger days.
>
> Non-stop pursuing of wealth will only turn a person into a twisted being, just like me.

Dear reader, pray for a good life to share with those we love before that final curtain. And may our lives end with the blessing of "fierce tears" and the final expletive: Oh wow. Oh wow. Oh wow.

TABLE OF CONTENTS

Chapter 1 **Pilgrims on the Gold Dirt Road in God's Country**

"I came so that you may have life and have it more abundantly!" (John 10:10).

Covid-19 has given us a chance to refocus our spiritual lives. We can choose to leave the weary soul sickness of life without hope and to focus on the Resurrection and God's promise of abundant life. Covid-19 has interrupted our journey, briefly, but we can continue heaven bound on the road all runners come. Many of us manage to travel carefree through our 30's, 40's and 50's. Then the "check engine" light starts flashing on occasion.

At 105 years Moshe suddenly stopped going to synagogue. His Rabbi asked, "How come we don't see you at services anymore?"

Moshe looked about and whispered, "I'll tell you, Rabbi. When I got to be 90, I expected God to take me any day. But then I got to be 95, 100, then 105. I figured God must have forgotten about me, and I don't want to remind him."

As a Baby-Boomer I assert that God has not yet forgotten us. I try to see the signs and hear God's promptings as I try to attune my ear to his Word. A new urgency exists today as Baby Boomers are retired or retiring; and in the U.S. alone, forty million people are sixty-five and older. This fact coupled with fear of dying from Covid-19 has caused near panic as everyone scrambles to find answers and hope in a world struggling with suffering and death.

I have noticed too that many of those who follow us, Generation X, Y and Z, are too busy to hear, too distracted to reflect, but too intelligent to ignore the calling of God. I have the uncomfortable feeling that sometimes all of us avoid the reality of our spiritual lives and the fact of death by immersing ourselves in our work and pursuits so that Sunday morning finds many of us not in church but at some *really worthwhile activity* involving family, our jobs or other noble pursuit.

Do not let Sunday be taken from you.
If your soul has no Sunday, it becomes an orphan.
- Albert Schweitzer

To my readers who are too intelligent to ignore God's calling, I present this book about our journey to the Father. I recall the opening lines of a novel that said there are some books into which the author should take the readers by the hand and gently lead them. Annie Dilliard asserts: "One should write as if posthumously .... Write as if you were dying. At the same time, assume you write for an audience consisting solely of terminal patients. That is, after all, the case."

We can joke about it, but in the end, we are all born with an expiration date. Death, it can be argued, came about after God's plan was adjusted to accommodate Adam and Eve's (our) failings. We are all in the plan. Some of us are more conscious of its unfolding and make deliberate adjustments. In the end we all hope to join the heavenly banquet where the wines are clear and well-aged (Isaiah 25:6). That is good news!

The Gold Dirt Road in God's Country

Before we get to that banquet, we have a road to travel. In some ways we must build that road and maintain it to keep our journey on course. I go the same journey as my father before me.

"Yorch is beelding heemself the road to heavin," my Norwegian neighbor said when my dad was a Counselor for the R.M. of Hearts Hill back in the 1940's. A two-mile stretch of road was under construction due west of my father's farm to St. Donatus, the stone church on the hill. That road continued to be the link to Church, and in a sense, heaven.

In the 1960's my brother-in-law, several of my brothers and I set out on a winter Saturday, with shovels and a car, to plow our way through the snow so that we would be able to get to Church Sunday morning. We kept the road for the first mile or so then had to head through the ditch and follow a line of hills to get around the low spots covered in drifts. My brother-in-law loved this challenge. No drift was made that could stop his Dodge!

The same stretch of road has seen wedding cars and funeral processions. It has seen gravel, and in later years, oiled top. As a child I remember traveling on it by horse-drawn cart in summer and beside it by sleigh in winter as we went to and from school. That stretch of road has seen blizzards and drought, grasshoppers and flood, speeding cars and pedestrians. I saw my father driving a horse-drawn box-wagon along-side that road and shoveling grasshopper-poison bait along the edge of the field on a dry, hot summer day to stop the pestilent plague that was hopping across that road.

Yes, the road is a metaphor for life. My parents, some siblings and in-laws have passed on to their reward. The struggles of life, of road building and plowing snow, will end as surely for you and for me. The question is: "Are we on the road to heaven?"

The little victories we win on the road to heaven are important: the efforts we make to get to Church on Sunday, the struggles against Mother nature and our natures, and the deeper reflections in moments of silence. My Dad and Mother did it! Others before us have done it. You and I, also, need to "beeld that road to heavin."

Pursuing the same metaphor in the twenty-first century, we are Pilgrims on the "gold dirt road", as the second line of Country and Western singer Blake Shelton's "God's Country" describes it. When I see the road from my father's farm to the church on the hill, I see a golden road where there used to be dust. It is a road that leads to everything, because this is God's country.

The solid philosophy in the song "God's Country" gives us direction and purpose. We work hard all week, pray for rain, grow grain for money, and we put it back on the plate in church on Sunday morning, because this is God's country. We share the bread Sunday, and the baptisms in holy water, and we're proud to be from God's country. We need to take this life and live it with enthusiasm, carrying our weaknesses on our way to meet the Lord.

Take this life and live it! Reminds me of Leonard Cohen's "Take this waltz, take this waltz. It's yours now. It's all that there is." Take this life, with its sensuality and beauty! Take this life and live it. All is gift from God. We need to take this life and live it, carrying our weaknesses with us as we go on our journey to meet the Lord. Sometimes we go "with a garland of freshly cut tears." (Cohen). We thank God when it's raining, and we see the light in the sunshine. (from "God's Country" Scott Johnson and Scott Hendricks).

We are all heaven bound as we travel the pilgrim road of this life. May we have the vision to see the gold in the dust on the road that seems to lead to nothing. Pilgrims travel on a path that is special to their faith. Normally the pilgrim on his journey takes time to pray, to spend time with God and to be freed from the concerns of everyday life. Often the pilgrim is looking for peace or healing, and to grow closer to God. And doesn't that describe our daily lives?

13

Chapter 2 Finding Jesus During Covid-1

The Grace of Christ's love still streams toward us from the eternal sacrifice of the Cross. The churches are reopening, and Jesus has not abandoned us.

Covid-19 is creating fear and panic as well as challenges for growth. Coronavirus has triggered suicides and fear of dying alone in isolation. The guilt and difficulty of grieving where traditional funerals are not possible make these painful times. Suicide hotline calls are up, but the spiritual upside is that we are experiencing a spiritual renaissance and a new hope in an immortal soul beyond this material world.

A Flowering Mysticism

During the Black Death of the fourteenth century the Franciscans saw, in the crucified Christ, God's entering into the suffering of humanity in order to redeem mankind. In this re-ordering of spirituality Medieval mystic Julian of Norwich claimed that Christ's emaciated and bloody body "resembled our foul, black death, which our fair, bright, blessed Lord bore for our sins." American theologian

Bernard McGinn described this fourteenth century spiritual growth as a *flowering mysticism.*

Today we see signs of renewed growth resulting from a forced spiritual reassessment. In "How God Is Acting Amid the Coronavirus Crisis" John Horvatt II, author of *Return to Order,* lists three positive outcomes from the suspension of services in the Catholic Church during Covid-19. The first is that the faithful pray more. Parents and families read spiritual books and find more time for prayer and contemplation. Their faith is growing! Some pray the rosary several times a day instead of just once. One person reported seeing the implications of his sins much more clearly.

A second positive outcome is increased contact with the family. Despite the hardships of unemployment, many family members are grateful for the extra time spent together. The third way the crisis is positive is that people report that their lives have slowed down: "We are enjoying the slower pace and the opportunity to be together more," wrote one mother.

It would be well to remember that "Pain and suffering do not have the final say over human existence. Instead, they become a means by which God redeems souls who, through prayer, follow the footsteps of the crucified." ("COVID-19 and the Spiritual Life", [Pentecostal Theologian] Dale M. Coulter, 4.14.20). As the medieval Black Death caused a resurgence of individual spirituality, so today we are invited to turn inward and find Christ, in our selves and in our homes. The isolation of Covid-19 distancing has prepared us for this task. Church closures have forced us to find Jesus in our homes instead of seeking him in church.

Even before Covid-19, church attendance was down. Now the coronavirus has presented us with an opportunity for spiritual reassessment. In the key area of spirituality, the state of our souls, we are in a time of forced soul-searching. We do not need to spend money to find a place of solitude or retreat. We are already stuck inside in isolation, the place where we can contemplate a growing mysticism. As ordinary Christians are forced, in part, to take charge of their own religious lives, we see potential for growth and renewal. At the risk of over-simplification, this is what appeared to happen after the Black Plague. Personal piety and lay movements led to a greater independence from monks and priests in the medieval times. The great intellectual resurgence that followed gave rise to the Renaissance.

Is Coronavirus a Chastisement for Sin?

An aftermath of the Black Death was the belief that sickness was a punishment for our sins. Is the coronavirus God's way of punishing our transgressions? It depends whom you ask. The honest and repentant sinner says yes. And that is probably closest to the truth. But God is a God of mercy. True, we should do penance for our sins, and this may often bring God's blessing rather than God's wrath.

The Medieval sense of repentance during the Black Death led to extreme behaviour. Flagellants wandered from town to town whipping themselves and each other with scourges. If the plague was a punishment from God, then their self-mutilation was a form of atonement. God does not exact extreme penitential measures from us. In his mercy, God chastises us, not because he desires to punish us, but because he wishes to deliver us from punishment. He wants to pardon and save us.

The Cross amid Covid-19 on Good Friday 2020 was a great opportunity for individual reflection on Christ's sacrifice and our sinful nature. In isolation we contemplated the mysteries of Christ's suffering. The mystery of the Passion of Christ continued to unravel for us. Why did Christ have to suffer as described in Isaiah 52:14: "his appearance was so disfigured beyond that of any human being and his form marred beyond human likeness"? Covid-19 gives us a hint.

This world seems to have come undone, and it is not the first time, as we know. We can choose to bear our crosses patiently, but it is so much easier if we know Christ is with us. On Good Friday and during the season of Lent we pondered the significance of the Cross of Christ. Good Friday is gone, and Covid-19 continues. Hopefully, we started to realize that carrying the cross of Covid-19 is a way to enter into the suffering of Christ. Jesus suffered and died so that he could enter into our suffering and our death. In fact, Jesus died a physical death. Then from the grave as God, he raised his physical body to join his Spirit and made possible our eventual Resurrection.

Why was all of this necessary? So that in his love Jesus could invite us to accept him as our Lord and Saviour. Will we let ourselves be so loved? Will we accept a sliver of the cross of suffering and pain in the work of redemption?

Our world was undone by the rebellion of human nature against God. We blame Adam and Eve, but we find many and original ways to sin. It is to redeem us and our nature that the sacrifice of Jesus continues. Original sin closed the gates of heaven to us. All of nature had to be redeemed, and God permitted the incarnation and redemption plan of salvation to unfold. Jesus' suffering on the cross shows us the evil nature of sin, so deserving of the wrath of God.

The reality of Satan and the cruelty of man was in evidence at Calvary. Here the Suffering Servant of Isaiah 53 became the Redeemer of mankind. Jesus saved us from all the punishment our sins deserve. Will we let ourselves be so loved? "For when we were yet without strength, in due time Christ died for the ungodly." (Romans 5:6). How can we not love Him, serve Him, obey Him, and worship Him now and forever, as we gaze upon the face of Him Who loved us so?

Until He comes for us, should we not endeavour to dwell in the house of the Lord and walk in the land of the living? If we let God lead our lives, we can enjoy life even on our worst days.

A New Easter

Christ is Risen!

Christ has conquered death and given us immortality. We are made for eternity. We have been released from the chains of mediocrity, sadness, hopelessness, fear, hunger, suffering and even death - and we are free!

Christ has risen and has opened for us the doors of Paradise; a place without coronavirus, but also without hatred, bitterness and enmities. A place of joy and happiness; homeland of Love, for which we are created.

Coronavirus cannot change the empty tomb. (ideas from Easter message of Dr. Gregory Mertz, CitizenGo Team and infectious disease specialist).

St Joseph and Pandemic Patron Saints

The church through the ages has brought healing and medicine, especially during times of plague and sickness. A model of service to the sick, St. Marianne Cope (1838-1918) answered the call of the king of Hawaii to bring her Sisters to Hawaii and serve the lepers alongside St. Damien of Molokai. Marianne assured her Sisters that not one of them would contract the deadly disease. The Sisters worked with the lepers of Molokai for nearly a century without one of them contracting the terrible disease.

We have closed the schools where prayer was banned, and we are subjected to the whims of the faithless, like the Mayor of Indiana who has replaced "Good Friday" with "Spring Holiday" on the calendar. Is it not time to turn back to God in penance and seek God's forgiveness and comforting peace? A good start when facing a contagious virus, pandemic or plague is to invoke the help of Jesus, Mary, Joseph and all the Saints. Also helpful is knowing which Saint has a vested interest in the particular malady.

As Canadians we are more familiar with St Andre of Quebec who brought about many miracles with his intercessory prayers to St Joseph, who happens to be the patron saint of Canada. I have seen the crutches piled up in St Joseph's Oratory. Wikipedia reports: "When an epidemic broke out at a nearby college, [St]André volunteered to nurse. Not one person died.

Let me share just a couple of examples of St Joseph's intervention in time of plague. A Mr. Augery implored St Joseph to help his young son when the surgeons had given him up for dead. They were carrying the boy to the pest-house for burial only to find him cured when they arrived. Nine other members of the family were saved from the plague as well. Tevenet, a good old man from a village near Lyons, infected with the plague, asked the vicar of the place whether there were any means for his recovery. The vicar answered him that there were none but by having recourse to St. Joseph, and by making a vow every year to keep his feast... The pious old man
20

immediately made the vow, and at the same time found himself freed from the plague.

There are stories of Mary's apparitions in Vicenza, Italy, and her interventions during the plagues of the fifteenth century. When the construction of a shrine began, the plague almost immediately stopped. Today the shrine of the Madonna of Monte Berico is visited by thousands.

As to what we should do to combat today's COVID-19, we need to follow the suggested guidelines to help reduce the spread of virus. In addition we need to be a voice of reason to stop panic and offer assistance to those most vulnerable.

Finally, we need to PRAY. We are in God's hands and God wants only the best for us and our loved ones. Times of crisis can bring us closer to the arms of our loving God. Join the many who have started intercessory prayers to end the scourge of this disease. The Rosary is a formidable weapon since our Mother Mary wants desperately to help us. Jesus longs for our embrace as well.

The Grace of Christ's love still streams toward us from the eternal sacrifice of the Cross. The churches are reopening, and Jesus has not abandoned us.

Chapter 3 Heaven Bound and the Eucharist

This world seems to have come undone with Covid-19, and it is not the first time, as we know. We can choose to bear our crosses patiently, but it is so much easier if we know Christ is with us.

The story is told of a noble man who died and his chief servant had the task of telling the other servants of their master's death. When he delivered the news one of the servants asked, "I wonder where he went."
"To heaven," said the other servants.
"I don't think so," said the chief servant.
"Why not?" they asked.
"Well, our master traveled a great deal, and whenever he went to a foreign land, he would spend time planning and packing and telling people where he was going. He never spoke about heaven," he said.

At a Centennial celebration of 100 years of Faith in the Archdiocese of Regina, I remember reflecting on the Faith of our Fathers and Mothers. I felt a close communion with my Mother and Dad and several siblings who have gone before us into heaven.

Words can't touch the experience of closeness to our loved ones we visit in this way. That is why our bodies choke us up so we can't sing or even speak. It is a time for being, for experiencing that love we share with our dear ones who will be there as part of the incredible joy of heaven.

We will know so many in heaven! Recently I thought that if I were in heaven this particular afternoon, I could visit with Elvis Presley. I've never had that opportunity. Heaven is one building Elvis will not leave.

Think of all the hints our creator gives us about heaven: sunshine, starlight, dancing, birdsong, clouds, landscape and the list is infinite! We will know in heaven! Heaven is something to talk about and plan for, but death will visit us first.

Father Robert McTeigue, SJ, wrote an article "Who wants to think about death? I do, and I want you to, and here's why". McTeigue goes on to share this witty remark by Samuel Johnson who was viewing the magnificent Palace of Versailles. "The trouble with a place like this is that it makes it too difficult to die." Nobody wants to contemplate suffering and dying while surrounded by the pleasures of this world.

McTeigue discusses a paradox about dying: "Death has been described as a terror, because it removes us from this world; it has been described as a mercy, because it removes us from this world." Saint and sinner tremble at the outcome. Triumph is there for the Christian and the person of virtue. There are unfathomable riches in the consoling rituals and graces afforded to us by the Church. Yet many of our churches are unusually empty on Sunday mornings. Small wonder we don't want to think about death. We are too busy with worldly things. "We will have time for that stuff later," the devil whispers in our ears. The good news is that the church can help us through that final portal on our way to meet the Lord. There are sacraments, including the anointing of the sick, and there are prayers of departure like this last blessing:

Through the holy mysteries of our redemption,
may almighty God release you
from all punishments in this life
and in the life to come.
May he open to you the gates of paradise
and welcome you to everlasting joy.
R. Amen.

Triumphant Hope

Thinking about death can give us the perspective to live a fuller life. Isn't God's plan revealed through his son's coming to earth remarkable? If we but understood God's plan for us at any point in this pilgrim journey to heaven, we would fall on our knees in awe and exclaim: "Wow! Oh wow!! Oh wow!" "Death is no more than falling blindly into the arms of God." (St. Maria Maravillas de Jesus). Let us explore this statement at a more personal level.

When my father was dying of pancreatic cancer, he asked my older brother Father Wendelin, a Roman Catholic priest, "What will it be like, waking up on the other side?" My father had always been the cornerstone of faith to me. He had always explained that we do not really die. We just awake on the other side. My father was there for us when my grandparents died. He sang the Requiem

24

funeral Masses at our little country church of St Donatus for many relatives and friends. Yet here he was, struggling with life's question. It is human to seek the answer to that question: what will it be like when we are born to eternal life?

The answer got me out of bed early on the first day of summer, 2019. It was dawn! At 4:38 I turned on the computer to record what I had been struggling with for the past hour. There was a picture of temples in Angkor, Cambodia, on the screen. "Like what you see?" the caption read. I did.

It was a sunset! Appropriately enough. "From certain spots you can gaze down on some of the world's most renowned temples," it said. "Come for the sunsets … stay for the thousand years of history."

Well my story was closer to two thousand years. I had been praying the Luminous Mysteries this night, as I often do when I awaken in the wee hours. I got to the Transfiguration, which precedes the Institution of the Eucharist mystery. And that is where it all started catching me.

Jesus took Peter, James and John up the mountain to pray. His face was changed, and his clothing became sparkling white. Moses and Elijah appeared in glory and were talking to him. Peter said, "Master, it is wonderful for us to be here; so let us make three shelters, one for you, one for Moses and one for Elijah." The voice of the Father spoke, "This is my Son, the Chosen One. Listen to him." (Luke 9:33, 35).

25

This all happened shortly before Jesus entered Jerusalem for the Passover. It was, in a sense, a preparation for his sharing of the greatest gift to us, the Eucharist, which prefigured his offering up his body and blood on the cross of Good Friday.

And it was a Good Friday! And it is a Good Friday! All our joy as Christians is predicated on our understanding of this mystery that gives life! "I came so that you may have life and have it more abundantly!" (John 10:10).

The final page of our lives will be a triumph if we turn to Jesus with the prayer of Dismas: Lord, remember me when you come into your Kingdom. To make our heaven bound journey easier, Jesus has provided the appropriate food, the bread of angels, that makes our triumphal journey possible.

The Eucharist and Our Journey

What if I told you there is a part of us that will never die? That at the moment of our deaths we can have Jesus inside us with the promise that we will live forever?

What is so important about the Eucharist? It was the culmination of the life of Jesus Christ as he moved from his birth to the cross. It is Christ's plan to be with us, to be food for our journey as we move through our pilgrimage, as we travel the road all runners come.

What do Christians believe about the eucharist? Most Christians generally recognize a special presence of Christ in this rite. Though Christians generally agree that there is no perceivable change in the bread and wine, Roman Catholics and Orthodox Christians believe that the bread and wine actually become the body and blood of Christ. Lutherans believe the true presence in a sacramental union. Reformed Christians believe in a real spiritual presence of Christ, while others believe in a symbolic reenactment of the Last Supper.

The actual or symbolic presence in the Eucharist is best viewed in the context of several scriptural verses. "The words I have spoken to you—they are full of the Spirit and life." (John 6:63). Jesus is called the Word of God who came to earth and was made flesh (John 1:14). The Word of God is also the Bread of Life (John 6:48). It is possible to understand this mystery of Christ's presence in the Eucharist in different ways and at different levels.

"Christian, remember your dignity, and know that you share in God's own nature, do not return by sin to your former base condition. Bear in mind who is your head and of whose body you are a member. Do not forget that you have been rescued out of darkness and brought into the light of God's kingdom." (St. Leo the Great, Christmas Sermon, 1).

A rewarding activity I enjoy as a lay minister is taking communion to the sick or shut ins. Here are God's holy people! They embrace the suffering and limitations of their state and all the while prepare for that final union with God. "When I think of the happiness that is in store for me, every sorrow, every pain becomes dear to me." (St Francis of Assisi).

One of these precious members of the Body of Christ used to greet me with, "I have been waiting for the communion." She waited until after her 100th birthday and is now with the Lord. I'm sure the Lord *was waiting* for her. As a representative of the Church I get to have a precious, short little visit with God's holy ones who are side-lined.

The Eucharist is the life within us that will never die! In so many ways the Gospel of John enunciates the fact that the Eucharist gives us life, Christ's life. And that life is eternal. That part in us will never die! "Whoever eats my flesh and drinks my blood lives in me and I live in that person …. Anyone who eats this bread will live forever." (John 6:56, 58).

Christ enlivens us and lives in us through the Word in our hearts and the light in our souls! "Anyone who loves me will keep my word, and my Father will love him, and we shall come to him and make a home in him." (John 14:23).

My father's question is answered. We *will* live as we awake on the other side. We will take with us the life of the Spirit as it has grown in us. We will take love with us, our good works, and enough joy to experience our birth into life. That is what makes joy in this life a choice we can make as we follow the road all runners come!

Chapter 4 Proof of Heaven

Covid-19 has generated a fear of death so universal that even avowed atheists have pondered the eternal and the possibilities of heaven. How are we to live with this fear? In "How Are We to Live in an Atomic Age?" C.S. Lewis said, "Why, as you would have lived in the sixteenth century when the plague visited London almost every year, or as you would have lived in a Viking age when raiders from Scandinavia might land and cut your throat any night; or indeed, as you are already living in an age of cancer."

We have our own list of mortal threats including Covid-19. Our situation is not novel, Lewis says. Death is not a chance; it is a certainty. If the atomic bomb is going to kill us, let it find us doing human things, "praying, working, teaching, reading, listening to music, bathing the children, playing tennis, chatting to our friends over a pint and a game of darts—not huddled together like frightened sheep and thinking about bombs."

Let us then live daily in the presence of God and choose a life sparkling with joy and hope. Faith is what makes happiness possible.

What is Heaven really like?

One of the best foods I have ever tasted is a recipe called "Death by Chocolate". Add rich creams, a chocolate mousse and caramel sauce to the best chocolate cake you have ever tasted, and you have an idea what I am about to describe. What is heaven like?

What was our first idea of heaven? As children we had various definitions. Heaven is the place where you can eat all the brown sugar lumps you want and still want more. Heaven is the place where you can eat all the ice cream you want without the headache. As we grew up our perceptions changed. Heaven is the place where you will meet Grandpa and Grandma again, or Uncle and Aunt. Heaven is the place where there will be no more pain and sorrow, no illness. We were getting closer to the truth.

I like St. Cyprian's description of Heaven as a great family reunion, where we hope to see many of our loved ones. Just step outside of TIME for a moment and savour this meeting. Walk about and mingle.

> *There a large number of dear ones are waiting for us, of parents, brothers, children; a numerous and full crowd are longing for us; already secure of their own immortality, and still anxious for our safety. To come to the sight and the embrace of these, how great will be the mutual joy to them and to us! What a pleasure of the kingdom of heaven is there without the fear of dying, and with an eternity of living! How consummate and never-ending a happiness!*

There is the glorious company of the apostles; there is the assembly of exulting prophets; there is the unnumbered family of martyrs crowned for the victory of their struggles and suffering; there are virgins triumphing, who, by the power of chastity, have subdued the lusts of the flesh and the body; there are the merciful recompensed, who with food and bounty to the poor have done the works of righteousness, who keeping the Lord's commands have transferred their earthly inheritance into heavenly treasures.

To these, O most dearly beloved brethren, let us hasten with most eager longing; let us desire that our lot may be to be with these speedily; to come speedily to Christ.

Thinking about this scene St Cyprian describes, it is with some reluctance that we come back from there. Think of hugging your parents, your spouse, your best friend, whoever it is who has been separated from you by death. Should we not live our short lives so that this reality will come about?

What did Jesus say about heaven? First of all, he taught us about ourselves. We are made in the image and likeness of God himself. Man has been given a sublime dignity based on the intimate bond which unites us with

31

our creator (Psalm 8). Heaven begins with these realizations on earth.

As we continue to listen to God we hear: "The people who walked in darkness have seen a great light; on those who live in a land of deep shadow a light has shone." (Isaiah 9:2-4); "The earth shall be full of the knowledge of the Lord as the waters cover the sea. On that day the root of Jesse [Christ the Lord] shall stand as a signal to the people; the nations shall inquire of him, and his dwelling shall be glorious." (Isaiah 11:9-10); and "Come to me, all who labor and are heavy burdened … and you will find rest for your souls." (Matthew 11:28-29). How much of heaven we are already enjoying! Living in *the light*. Seeing signs and wonders. Resting our troubles in Jesus at times of difficulty.

Let me illustrate how living in God's Kingdom works. An anthropologist studying the social behavior of the children of an African tribe proposed a game. He put a fruit basket underneath a tree and said whoever reached the basket first could have all the fruit. When he said, "Go," the children joined hands and reaching the basket, sat down in a big circle and shared the fruits. The anthropologist asked why they did not try to get the prize for themselves. They replied, "Ubuntu, how can one of us be happy if all the others are sad?"

As Christians we are all members of one body that is Christ on earth. True, we are still growing and becoming that part of Christ, but we must daily realize our role in making that Kingdom come. *How can any one of us be happy if all the others are sad?* Archbishop Desmond Tutu says about the South African concept of *ubuntu*: "[It] means my humanity is caught up, is inextricably bound up, in theirs. We belong in a bundle of life." Simply, I am because we are.

We pray most frequently, *"Thy Kingdom come."* How do we understand that Kingdom? How does it work? In God's Kingdom, surely, all will be love and sharing. God's longing to love us and touch us is reflected in the lives of special saints. God is constantly reaching out to us if we are attuned to his word, his calling.

As St Phillip Neri begged for the gifts of the Holy Spirit on the eve of Pentecost, in the catacomb of San Sebastiano. A small ball of fire descended, entered his mouth and went to his heart. Phillip experienced such an intense love that he fell to the ground in ecstasy crying, "Enough, enough, Lord, I can bear no more."

God, in his great love for us, sent Jesus to unravel the mystery. 1 John 3:2 tells us, "We are already God's children … when he appears, we shall be like Him." Jesus has appeared and we are invited *to be* part of that Kingdom daily. Jesus tell us, "The Kingdom of God is in your midst." (Luke 17:21). The coming of that Kingdom cannot be observed (17:21). People will not see it and say, "Here it is". But Jesus explains what the Kingdom of God is like in successive parables in Matthew 13. In the mustard seed and yeast parables Jesus tells us how the Kingdom will grow in us, and in turn, how we will grow in community until all of us share that common love that makes up the recognizable body of Christ on earth. We cannot be happy if everyone else is sad.

God's love for us is so simple. Remember what it was like to play with your parents? Rolling on the floor, tickling each other, brought you so close! That is how God loves us. That is why God sent Jesus to share experiences with us - so we can see the Father's love and touch that love! The Kingdom is around us. We can touch it, and God can touch us. Thanks be to our Brother Jesus who exemplifies what the Kingdom is like. Jesus is God's loving presence with us. Ubuntu. We are because He is.

Proof of Heaven

I was chatting with a friend during the Easter season who had lost his mother in the past year. Easter seemed more sombre to him. He said, "No one has come back from the dead to tell us about what is there." I corrected him by suggesting that *one* did come back to us. Jesus ate and drank with the disciples in his risen body (Acts 10:37).

Pope Benedict XVI said, "The Resurrection of Christ is our hope!" This the Church proclaims with joy. She announces the hope that is now firm and incontrovertible. What a great life we can have if we are sure of a rewarding afterlife. How can we be sure there is heaven after Death?

I like this version of a story about twins talking to each other in the womb:

> The sister said to the brother, "I believe there is life after birth."
> Her brother protested vehemently,

"No, no, this is all there is. This is a dark and cozy place, and we have nothing else to do but to cling to the cord that feeds us."

The little girl insisted, "There must be something more than this dark place. There must be something else, a place with light where there is freedom to move." Still she could not convince her twin brother.

After some silence, the sister said hesitantly, "I have something else to say, and I'm afraid you won't believe that, either, but I think there is a mother."

Her brother became furious. "A mother!" he shouted. "What are you talking about? I have never seen a mother, and neither have you. Who put that idea in your head? As I told you, this place is all we have. Why do you always want more? This is not such a bad place, after all. We have all we need, so let's be content."

The sister was quite overwhelmed by her brother's response and for a while didn't dare say anything more. But she couldn't let go of her thoughts, and since she had only her twin brother to speak to, she finally said, "Don't you feel these squeezes every once in a while? They're quite unpleasant and sometimes even painful."

"Yes," he answered. "What's special about that?"

"Well," the sister said, "I think that these squeezes are there to ready us for another place, much more beautiful than this, where we will see our mother face-to-face. Don't you think that's exciting?"

The brother didn't answer. He was fed up with the foolish talk of his sister and felt that the best thing would be simply to ignore her and hope that she would leave him alone.

Thus, while the one raved and despaired, the other resigned herself to birth and placed her trust in the hands of her mother. Hours turned into days, and days into weeks. Soon it was time. They both knew their birth was at hand, and they both feared what they did not know.

As the one was first to be conceived, so he was first to be born, the other following. They cried as they were born into the light. They coughed out fluid and gasped the dry air. And when they were sure they had been born, they opened their eyes – seeing life after birth for the first time. What they saw was the beautiful eyes of their mother, as they were cradled lovingly in her arms. They were at home. (Author Unknown)

This story may help us to think about death in a new way. We can live as if this life were all we had, as if death were absurd and we had better not talk about it; or we can choose to claim our divine childhood and trust that death is the painful but blessed passage that will bring us face-to-face with our God.

Most of us need more convincing that there is a God and a heaven than a "feel good" story, no matter how touching. One of the best examples of proof to the most doubting scientific and rational mind is that related by Doctor Eben Alexander in *Proof of Heaven.*

"The idea of near-death experiences (NDE) of heaven and God are 'wonderful stuff', but in my opinion, pure fantasy," Dr. Eben Alexander said before the encounter that changed his life. A neurosurgeon for twenty-five years, Eben contracted a deadly E. coli bacterial meningitis that left him in a coma for seven days. Despite the severity of the disease with a mortality rate of 97%, the prayers and faith of his family and friends helped bring about what many describe as a miracle of healing.

But all seemed hopeless as his loved ones surrounded him one last time. He was dying. Michael made one last impassioned plea:

"Lord, bring Eben back to us. I know it's in your power."

Sylvia and Bond looked into the eyes that had been "Staring dead and unmoored, askew like those of a broken doll." Suddenly, his eyes opened. Sylvia shrieked. And Eben's eyes began to look around.

Amazing as his survival was his complete mental recovery. The first thing Eben did was record all the details of his journey into heaven and the Divine encounter. Later he read books on NDE to discover common truths.

In Elizabeth Kubler Ross's *On Life After Death* a twelve-year-old describes a NDE to her father "about travelling to an indescribable landscape full of love and beauty, and how she met and was comforted by her brother ... The only problem, the girl told her father, 'is that I don't

37

have a brother'."

Tears filled the father's eyes. He told her about the brother who died just three months before she was born.

After his NDE Eben sees the picture of his birth sister he has never met. His eyes mist. She looks strangely, hauntingly familiar. They had often said she was kind, practically an angel. And Eben's guide journeying through the eternal realm had been "a beautiful girl with cheekbones and deep blue eyes ... peasant clothes ... riding along on a patterned surface – the wing of a butterfly ... guiding him through the places and processes to universes whose center was love and where all questions were answered instantly in an explosion of light."

"But now there was no mistaking her, no mistaking the loving smile, the confident and infinitely comforting look, the sparkling blue eyes. It was she. [His girl on a butterfly wing who guided him in the place where the higher and lower worlds met was his sister]."

In *Proof of Heaven* Dr. Eben Alexander expresses his absolute inability to explain the "richly interactive experiential tapestry" of his near-death experience. Eben was led to his ultimate realization: "I needed to completely embrace my role as doctor, as a scientist and healer, and as the subject of a very unlikely, very real, very important journey into the Divine itself."

Part of Eben's experience was to know absolutely that he was loved, that we are loved by our Creator. Because of his experiences Eben co-founded *Eternea* "to advance research, education, and applied programs concerning Spiritually transformative experiences, as well as the physics of consciousness and the interactive relationship between consciousness and physical reality". (From *PROOF OF HEAVEN* by Eben Alexander, M.D.

Many of us need more convincing. Indeed, if someone came back from the dead we might repent (Luke 16:30). God keeps sending us more evidence for conversion. Still we struggle with the paradoxes faith and doubt present us.

"Without somehow destroying me in the process, how could God reveal himself in a way that would leave no room for doubt? If there were no room for doubt, there would no room for me." - Frederick Buechner

"Where there is no longer any opportunity for doubts, there is no longer any opportunity for faith." -Paul Tournier

Human nature is such that we are hard to convince, even if the proof of heaven were to come from God himself. The story is told of:

Four rabbis who had a theological argument, and three were in accord against the fourth. "Three to one, majority rules," they argued.

"I know I'm right," the fourth said and asked God for a sign from heaven. A storm cloud rumbled and dissolved. But they were not convinced. The fourth prayed, "Please, God, a bigger sign!"

39

Four storm clouds appeared, rushed together and a bolt of lightning slammed into a tree. But the three insisted this could all be explained by nature. The sky turned black, the earth shook, and a deep voice boomed,   "HEEEEEEEE'S RIIIIIIIGHT!"

"Well," said the fourth Rabbi.

One of the three shrugged, "So, now it's three to two."

Death and what comes next is the point of a Clint Eastwood movie *Hereafter*. While Eastwood's movies have sent many characters to their graves, in *Hereafter* Eastwood ponders about where they actually went. "I've talked to people who claim to have had near-death experiences and they paint a picture, but I don't know," Eastwood said. "I mean, I just haven't been there. I don't intend to go there before my time … Does it exist? I don't know."

In the real world, when Jesus walked this earth with us, he enabled faith partly through the working of miracles. These did not stop with Christ's Ascension into heaven. In fact, Jesus promised that his Spirit would remain with us and in us and enable the continuation of more marvellous events, providing we have Faith. In the next chapter, let us look at just some of the more contemporary miracles that can strengthen our trust in God's plans for us.

Chapter 5 Miracles, Angels and Heaven Revealed

Miracles

We are living in a world that does not readily believe in miracles. If today we saw God part the red Sea with a strong wind, producing dry ground, would the world believe it?

In a BBC News story published January 8, 2020, David Jeffrey relates how residents of a small Australian beach town were prepared to jump into the sea in order to escape the roaring flames. "We could hear the roar. It sounded like a thousand freight trains coming at us. Then a huge gust, like someone had opened the door of a furnace, pushed us," Jeffery said. Then he and two other Christian believers began to pray. "We were going to die," Jeffery said. "Lord if you don't push this [fire] back now, we need [wind] from the east."

"As soon as I said that, it started blowing from the east a little bit. Then I got louder and [the wind] got stronger. Then I got louder again, and it got stronger again. I felt it change. I noticed that the bolder I got, the stronger [the wind got]. I was yelling, 'In Jesus' name, thank you Lord for rescuing these souls. Push it back Lord, rescue us!'"

"What God did was push [the fire] back from the east, which was impossible, but he did it. He did that for five minutes, which broke [the fire front] enough to stop it from getting to where we were," he said.

Jeffery relates a second miracle as he and his fellow residents were able to see the fire wall move toward people's homes — toward the Wave Oasis. "Then I heard God say to me, 'pray'. I started off with a pathetic little prayer," he said. "Then within me, this faith rose up and said, 'who are you praying to?' And I thought, 'Yes! You're the God of the Bible. Nothing's impossible with you! You've got angels Lord, put them at the corners of the property.'"

A second time, God did the impossible for the people of Mallacoota. Jeffery wants people to know that "there is a God and he does love them, that the only safe place is behind that cross."

Many today have encountered one miracle story or another. Some are especially close to the event that defies the laws of nature. Window washer Alcides Moreno, who plunged forty-seven stories and survived, became a believer in miracles. Moreno's brother was killed in the event and Alcides needed twenty-four pints of blood, was in a coma for seventeen days and woke up and spoke on December 24, 2007.

Doctors said that after falling above ten stories, patients usually go to the morgue, though one patient survived a nineteen story fall, less than half the distance Moreno fell. (from *New York Times* story).

An example of faith working with medicine is the story of physician and Pastor Tom Renfro who was dying of lymphoma. After much prayer from his faith group, Renfro said God told him it was time to go to the hospital for treatment. Chemotherapy was started and within forty-eight hours the tumours which were literally killing him softened and started disappearing. Eighteen years later Renfro is still testifying about this faith and medicine cure.

Our journey down life's narrow road is going to be better with God's continued presence. God is not indifferent to our need for faith and trust. Indeed, God sends us many miracles along the way. It is best not to be too full of our self importance and pride to notice. I'm reminded of a little story:

> *A man had been reading a book on self-image and when he arrived home that night he said to his wife, "From now on, I want you to know that I am the man of this house, and my word is law! Now prepare me a gourmet meal, and a sumptuous dessert. Then, after dinner, draw me my bath so I can relax. And when I'm finished with my bath, guess who's going to dress me and comb my hair?"*
>
> *"The funeral director," said his wife.*

Tapping spiritual sources close to us will put us in touch with many stories of the presence of Jesus or even angels among us. I recall an incident as a child when I fell into a washout filled with spring floods. In what seemed a split second I was whisked to solid ground, as if by an invisible hand.

Stories of Christ's presence in the Eucharist are perhaps the most amazing and surprisingly frequent. The miracle at Lanciano is perhaps best known, where the host that is Christ's body actually turned into flesh. Scientific tests have determined it to be heart tissue. And this flesh knows no decay even after 1200 years.

Another miracle happened at Ettiswil where a sacred host was stolen and taken from the church. The would-be thief (member of a satanic cult) later said it became too heavy to carry, so the young thief dropped it into a near-by nettle bush. The host was found, lifted high up and surrounded by a vivid light. It was divided into seven pieces that were united to look like a flower.

Closer to home and the present is the 1996 Eucharistic miracle at Buenos Aires. Here on August 18, as Fr. Alejandro Pezet was saying Holy Mass, a woman told him she had found a discarded host at the back of the church. Fr. Alejandro put the Host into a container of water in the tabernacle. This is a practise that allows the host to dissolve so it can be disposed of by returning it to nature.

On Monday, August 26, he saw to his amazement that the Host had turned into a bloody substance. He informed Cardinal Jorge Bergoglio, now Pope Francis. For several years this event was kept a secret until Bergoglio set up an extensive investigation.

Startling and real: Dr. Frederic Zugiba, cardiologist and forensic pathologist, testified that the analyzed material was a fragment of the heart muscle found in the wall of the left ventricle close to the valves. The large number of white blood cells indicated that the heart was alive at the time the sample was taken. (*absoluteprimacyofchrist.org*)

Not only did the tissue prove to be alive and of a male human heart, but DNA tests revealed that it was from the same human source as the Lanciano tissue of more than 1300 years before. The Catholic Church is still sorting out the facts involved and moving in the cautious manner of habit, but the startling facts can enrich our faith in the

44

Eucharist. Jesus Christ, body and blood, is alive and present to nourish us as we minister to others. And Jesus wants us to recognise his presence in a special way in the Eucharist.

It is a challenge to our Christian churches to work out the details. The Body of Christ is Christ's gift to nourish us all, to build his very life in us. Eternal life has begun inside us. The part of us that is Christ will never die. It is as St Augustine said, "We become what we eat."

The Body of Christ in the Eucharist is an invitation to all: "Take this and eat it, for this is my body." (Matthew 26:26). "Whoever eats of this bread will live forever." (John 6:54).

Let me share a couple of additional miraculous stories closer to home. *Spirit Daily* tells the story of a New York fireman who had a drinking problem and was overdoing it at an annual firemen's picnic upstate. Intoxicated, he'd wandered up a training platform, and before he knew it was stumbling off, ready to plummet several stories below.

At the last moment, as he tumbled off, he said a hand grabbed his and yanked him back up onto the platform with one amazing motion. To his astonishment he was looking at a stranger who was a mirror image of himself, but dressed far more neatly and very clean-shaven, far different than the dishevelled fireman. It was as if this mysterious angel was showing him how he could and should be. The mysterious man simply disappeared immediately after.

I have had the privilege of hearing a personal testimony of Father Milton McWatch, the first full-blood native Canadian ordained into the priesthood. His inspiring story of how the Lord led him, through difficulties that included residential school abuse, to ministry in the church moved many of us deeply.

On one occasion Christ appeared to him with the crown of thorns imbedded in his head. Milton wanted to remove a thorn, but Jesus would not permit it. Another time Christ appeared as a warrior who grabbed Milton by the heart.

Father Milton's encounters with Christ are as real and believable as the psychological and physical scars he still bears. Through all this a loving Christ has been present to Milton just as He wants to be present in our lives.

In *Sacred Heart, Gateway to God* Wendy Wright speaks of mystical realities that reinforce our faith beliefs. In that layered reality, that transcends the confines of space and time, dwell unseen presences of God and the saints.

Theologian Father Ron Rolheiser says of Wright's ideas, "What she describes here so brilliantly points towards something that is all but lost in our world today, namely, the fact that reality is more than just physical, that it has layers that we do not perceive empirically, that these layers are just as real as the physical, and there is more mystery within ordinary life than meets the eye. Mysticism is as real as science." (from "A Mystical Imagination").

It is, in the end, a question of FAITH. If we allow the Lord to enable our mystical imagination and allow Grace to work in us, a new world of the Spirit will open to us. The best way to do this is literally to be in Communion with Christ.

Of the Eucharist, Christ's body and blood, Jesus assures us: "I am the bread of life. He who comes to me will never be hungry … and I will raise him up on the last day … He who eats my flesh and drinks my blood lives in me and I live in him." (John 6:35, 54, 56).

St. John Vianney exhorted his parishioners to frequent communion: "Go to communion … go to Jesus with love and confidence … It is true, you are not worthy of it, but you need it … Do not say that you are sinners … and for that reason you do not dare approach it. I would as soon hear you say that you are very ill, and therefore you will not take any remedy, nor send for the physician." (*The Word Among Us*, September 2005, p.31).

As sinners we are in the privileged and powerful position to turn to God in the most pleasing way. Like the Centurion in Luke 7:1-10 we can say: Lord I am not worthy to have you come under my roof, but only say the word and I shall be healed. And Jesus, who was astonished at the Centurion's faith and healed his servant instantly, will surely reward our faith as readily and bring us healing and strength.

God is always ready to surprise us if we have even a little faith. In 2002 a nephew of mine, who happens to be my God son, hit a train in the dark of night. His truck was absolutely demolished. His mother emailed me a picture of it. It was hardly recognizable as a truck – pieces missing and crushed like a tin can. One of the clean-up crew asked, "How many people were killed in this collision?"

Several days after the accident, my nephew confided that two men had pulled him from the truck and placed him in the ditch. He did not see their faces. A passing motorist picked him up some time later. There was no trace of the two men. His injuries were superficial – some facial cuts, loose teeth and bruises. He was back at work within days.

I have a feeling my nephew's Grandfather (my Father-in-law) played a role in the incident. While my

Father-in-law was dying, his youngest son was working in a gold mine up north. The son recounts how he saw his dad in the mine the same day of his death. His father was wearing his black, chequered shirt, the same shirt we removed from the hospital when we collected his personal effects.

I want to share one more story to illustrate proof of heaven. Suppose you asked someone who was dying to give you a sign that they arrived on the other side. What would happen? My niece shared this story some years after her mother, my sister, was born to eternal life.

> Fifteen years ago today, my life took a drastic and devastating turn. It was on that day that my mom told me that her stomach cancer was terminal. Along with being heartbroken, I was mad; how unfair. I was twenty-seven and I wasn't ready to lose my mom. As the months passed and mom slowly regressed from eating small meals, to soft foods, to soup, to baby food, to being attached to an I-V. My family and I got mad with God. How could He let this happen to someone who had never hurt another living person? It was all so wrong.
>
> During that time we were having Mass at our farm almost daily, praying for my mom and others who were suffering from cancer. And did I feel like a hypocrite. I didn't even know if I wanted to believe in a God who could be so cruel. My older brother finally asked my mom, on one of her last days, how come she wasn't mad at God

and why she still prayed to God. My mom told my brother that it was okay to be mad at God, but her faith in God was the only thing she would take with her when she left. She would have to leave behind her husband of almost thirty-four years, her sixteen children and one grandchild, her award-winning garden and the house my dad and she built from the ground up. She just thought it would be better to take something with her, than go empty handed to her next life. So my mom's faith never faltered, and she took it with her.

Three months later, August 5, at 3:30 in the morning, five days shy of her fifty-seventh birthday, my mom went to her eternal reward. As my family and I drove back to the hospital to be with dad at 4:00 that morning, in the barley field across the road from our family farm fireworks were going off. We told dad about the fireworks when we arrived at the hospital and he mentioned how he had told mom just before she passed away to give him a sign when she got to heaven. Those fireworks must have been her sign. You see our farm is ten km from the nearest town and 100 km from the nearest city, so the odds were pretty slim that we would see fireworks at the particular moment.

You may ask do I still question my faith and doubt there's a God? Absolutely, it's only natural, but then I notice a little miracle here or there. Fireworks going off for no apparent reason, a single beautiful orange tiger lily (my mom's favourite flower) among the purple and white orchids on the altar of my sister's wedding last summer. And my faith is restored and strengthened yet again.

And my niece added this little prayer to her story:

Let us pray!
In the name of the Father, the Son and Holy Spirit -
Father we ask you to give us eyes to see, ears to hear, and hearts to believe in the Miracles you show us everyday.
Thank you, Lord, for standing by us in our human weakness. Thank you, for the little miracles in life, that remind us You are always there. God Bless all our moms, those here with us and those there with You!
In the name of the Father, the Son and the Holy Spirit. Amen
Bishop James Mahoney, Mom and All the saints, pray for us!
Happy Mother's Day Mom.

How sure am I that there is a heaven beyond the sun? Like Job I want to express it in the strongest terms: "O that my words were written down! O that they were inscribed in a book! O that with iron pen and with lead they were engraved on a rock forever!" (Job 19:21-27). Job is so absolutely certain of the fact that there is an eternal life. He goes on: "For I know that my Redeemer lives, and that at the last he will stand upon the earth … in my flesh I shall see God."

If we follow the signs and recall the events of our salvation story, we can be certain of life after death. When we have doubt, it is because we have forgotten our stories of salvation. We need to visit scripture daily, and we need to be attuned to the daily workings of God around us.

Angels

God has provided us with assistance on our journey to heaven in the presence of Angels in our lives. It often seems children are closer to angels than adults. It is interesting to see how children perceive angels. What is fascinating about how children describe angels is that there are truths in some of their perceptions. Children were asked to write what they know about angels:

· When an angel gets mad, he takes a deep breath and counts to ten. And when he lets out his breath, somewhere there's a tornado. ~ Daniel, 7

· My angel is my grandma who died last year. She got a big head start on helping me while she was still down here on earth. ~ Amber, 9

· It's not easy to become an angel! First, you die. Then you go to heaven, and then there's still the flight training to go through. And then you got to agree to wear those angel clothes. ~ Matthew, 9

· Angels have a lot to do and they keep very

51

busy. If you lose a tooth, an angel comes in through your window and leaves money under your pillow. Then when it gets cold, angels go north for the winter. ~ Sara, 6

· My guardian angel helps me with math, but he's not much good for science. ~ Harry, 7

· Angels don't eat, but they do drink milk from Holy Cows! ~ Jerri, 5

· Angels talk all the way while they're flying you up to heaven. The main subject is where you went wrong before you got dead. ~ Ronald, 10

· I only know the names of two angels. Hark and Harold. ~ Gregory, 5

· Angels live in cloud houses made by God and his son, who's a very good carpenter. ~ Jacob, 6

· What I don't get about angels is why, when someone is in love, they shoot arrows at them. ~ Sarah, 7

· Some of the angels are in charge of helping heal sick animals and pets. And if they don't make the animals get better, they help the child get over it. ~ Randy, 9
(Internet source)

Then there are adult perceptions about angels:

• The reason that angels can fly is because they take themselves lightly. -G.K. Chesterton.

• You'll meet more angels on a winding path than on a straight one. -Daisey Verlaef.
• Don't drive faster than your angel can fly! -English Proverb
• We are like children, who stand in need of masters to enlighten us and direct us; and God has provided for this, by appointing his angels to be our teachers and guides. -Saint Thomas Aquinas
• We shall find peace. We shall hear angels; we shall see the sky sparkling with diamonds. -Anton Chekov
• These things I warmly wish for you: Someone to love, some work to do, A bit o' sun, a bit o' cheer, And a guardian angel always near. -Irish Blessing

There are biblical references to Angels and their role in our salvation history:
Jesus said, "Take care that you do not despise one of these little ones; for I tell you, their angels continually see the face of my Father in heaven." (Matthew18:10).

"Do not neglect hospitality, for through it some
    have unknowingly entertained
        angels." (Hebrews 13:2).

In life's most serious moments we call on the angels:

"May flights of angels lead you on your way
    to paradise and heavens eternal day!
May martyrs greet you after death's dark night

and bid you enter into Zion's light!
May choirs of angels sing you to your rest
with once poor Lazarus, now forever blest"

(from Latin hymn "In Paradisum" traditionally sung at funeral Masses before the body is taken out of the church for burial).

On October 2 more than a billion Catholics celebrate the feast of the Guardian Angels. Catholic theology teaches that we have angels to watch over us throughout our lives.

As a child I learned this simple prayer:

Angel of God, my guardian dear
To whom God's love commits me here
Ever this day be at my side
To light to guide, to rule and guard, Amen.

It was fitting that I prayed this every night as I grew up. On my wedding night, we were deciding what night prayers to say before falling asleep with my bride, and this angel prayer was still first on our list.

Saint John XXIII wrote: "Our Father in heaven has charged his angels to come to our assistance during our earthly journey … so that, protected by the angels' help and care, we may avoid the snares upon our path, subdue our passions, and … follow always the straight and sure road that leads to paradise."

True friends are like angels. They are
precious and rare, and false friends are like leaves,
found everywhere. -Unknown

On Christmas Eve and on other special occasions we can practically hear the Angels sing. The popularity of angels in our society today is unprecedented, especially if you happen to be married to one or you are from Annaheim. All joking aside, angels are popular in fiction and reality.

Angels accompany us at the end of life. We do not die alone. As my mother lay dying in her hospital bed, all of a sudden she fixed her eyes beyond us in the room, smiled, and radiated such a joy that I knew it was not caused by the presence of my wife and me. My wife had a similar experience when her father was on his deathbed. Stories of these phenomena are common.

Angels have played a significant role in how God has revealed himself to us. Gabriel announced the birth of John the Baptist to Zachary (*Luke* 1:11-20) and the conception, birth and mission of Jesus to Mary (*Luke* 1:26-38). The Archangel Michael is known as the protector of the Church and the angel who will be there to escort us into heaven at the moment of death. Even Shakespeare was aware of this role of the angels. When Hamlet is dying Horatio says, "Good night sweet prince, / And flights of angels sing thee to thy rest." (*Hamlet* V. ii. 350-351).

Popular fiction gives us a similar story about the presence of God's angels, especially at the moment of death. In an episode of *Touched by An Angel*, a mother is talking to the Angel of Death and says: "Are you some kind of angel? Well you're too late. Why didn't you do something?" He replies, "I did. I took her home. She was never alone."

Another exciting story from scripture tells how the men flinging Shadrack, Meshack and Abednego into the fiery furnace fell and died from the heat. King

Nebuchadnezzar sees four figures in the furnace, walking about, singing and praising God. The fourth was an angel who protected them so that not a hair was scorched, and they did not even smell of smoke. (*Daniel* 1:7).

Even Jesus had angels ministering to him. After he endured temptation by the devil, "angels appeared and looked after him." (Matthew 4:11). We have Christ's assurance that from infancy on we have angels to look after us: "Their [children's] angels in heaven are continuously in the presence of my Father in heaven." (Matthew 18:10).

Perhaps the most consoling thought about the moment of death is that we will not die alone. Our guardian angels and Michael the Archangel will be with us, and the gentle hands of our Creator will be ready to receive us as we are born into eternal life: "Do not fear, for I am with you." (Isaiah 10:1).

Revealing Heaven

In the beginning God wanted to share the joy of heaven with us, so he created us. It is good to think of what it is that he wanted to share with us. Since our minds are limited, we cannot fathom the mysteries not yet revealed to us. Those who have been to heaven and have come back have a better idea. We need to ponder for a while how much this God loves us! The whole plan of the incarnation and redemption was out of love for us! Amen! Amen! And Amen!

Some of the mystery of the afterlife has been revealed to us in various near-death experiences that have been recorded in convincing fashion. One of the more recent is that of a young boy who emerges from life-saving surgery with remarkable stories of his visit to heaven. In *Heaven Is for Real* four-year old Colton Burpo, son of a Nebraska pastor, slips into unconsciousness and enters heaven. There he meets God and various family members who have died previously. The movie version is very convincing as actual events in the life of this believable family support many theological truths about heaven.

The Saints have grasped the joy heaven promises perhaps better than most of us. Here are a few of their perceptions. St. Faustina wrote extensively about her spiritual travels to both paradise and perdition in her diaries, which have been endorsed by the Church as approved revelations. Her visions of hell have also received much attention. But I don't want to go there. Of heaven, she writes: "Today I was in heaven, in spirit, and I saw its unconceivable beauties and the happiness that awaits us after death. I saw how all creatures give ceaseless praise and glory to God. I saw how great is happiness in God, which spreads to all creatures, making them happy; and then all the glory and praise which springs from this happiness returns to its source; and they enter into the depths of God, contemplating the inner life of God, the Father, the Son, and the Holy Spirit, whom they will never comprehend or fathom. This source of happiness is unchanging in its essence, but it is always new, gushing forth happiness for all creatures."

God's plan is to share heaven with us. St Theresa of Liseux said, as glorious as heaven is, God finds the presence of his children infinitely more desirable: "Our Lord does not come down from heaven every day to lie in a golden ciborium. He comes to find another heaven which is infinitely dearer to him—the heaven of our souls, created in his image, the living temples of the adorable Trinity."

Scripture has given us glimpses of what heaven will be like. "Eye has not seen, nor ear heard, nor the heart of man imagined, what God has prepared for those who love him." (1 Corinthians 2:9). We will be like the risen body of Christ: "The Lord Jesus Christ … will transform our lowly body to be like his glorious body." (Philippians 3:20-21). We will shine like the sun (Matthew 13:43). All tears will be wiped away and all pain gone. Mourning and death shall be no more (Revelation 21:4).

There are the many rooms in the Father's house (John 14:2). That's where we will see all our long-lost family and friends. I will see my Godparents again. And I hope to see my ancestors who kept the faith in Russia.

And of course, there is the Isaiah 25 banquet scene with the well-aged wines. This is a place to pause and enjoy the Lord's favour. But there is time for all that since we shall not sleep (1 Corinthians 15:51). This will come in the twinkling of an eye. Time is another dimension that changes in heaven.

Chapter 6

God's Love and A Wonderful Life vs. Fear of Death

Fear of death from Covid-19 needs to be addressed relative to other mortal threats. As of January 19, 2021, there are 95.7 million cases world wide and over 2 million deaths. We are more used to other mortal risks like traffic accidents, heart attack or cancer, but the Covid-19 risk has us reeling. We can move forward still appreciating God's love and gifts.

Elizabeth Barrett Browning wrote:

> Earth's crammed with heaven,
> And every common bush aflame with God.
> But only those who see take off their shoes.
> The rest sit around and pluck blackberries.

Imagine meeting Jesus right after this life is over. Jesus asks, "Well, how was it?" And you reply, "Except for the last five minutes, it was pretty awesome."

Imagine with me for a moment a life lived with the level eyes of faith and not that of the hollow men Eliot describes who wake in that other kingdom sightless, with lips that form prayers to broken stone. Faith makes such a wonderful life possible. Living a faith-filled life takes away the fear and sting of death.

I was blessed in my life with parents and grandparents who had strong faith. Back in Russia, my Grandfather wanted to be a priest, but he was told, "No, you're strong enough to work." And work he did with the young family he brought with him to Saskatchewan. When my older brother was studying to be a priest he met with my Grandfather at my oldest brother's wedding. "Do you think you will become a priest?" he asked. My brother replied, "Everything looks promising." Then grandfather said, "If only it will come to pass." He shook my brother's hand for the last time and walked away. I was told later that he wept. Two days later he died suddenly.

Through his tears of joy Grandfather Rolheiser saw how my brother's vocation to the priesthood would impact the spirituality of the family in the next generation and the generations to come. The faith of our German-Russian fore-fathers that had survived 148 years in Russia would bear fruit in Canada. In the same way my father's faith was passed on to us. Recalling the emotion he felt as his son celebrated his first Mass in the country church, my Dad told him, "I didn't see you. Every time I looked at the altar [from the choir loft], my eyes blurred."

My parents and grandparents knew what it was like to stand on holy ground. They experienced moments of faith and communed with their God on a regular basis. When they met God on that first day in heaven they were not strangers. They frequently spent time with God. Their marriages had been blessed as had the marriage at Cana. Of this miracle Ben Franklin says, "We hear of the conversion of water into wine at the marriage in Cana as of a miracle. But the conversion is, through the goodness of God, made every day before our eyes. Behold the rain which descends from heaven upon our vineyards, and which incorporates itself with the grapes, to be changed into wine; constant proof [there's a pun in here somewhere] that God loves us and loves to see us happy."

"Let us now sing the praises of
our ancestors in their generations.
Some of them have left behind a name,
So that others declare their praise.
These were Godly people,
Whose righteous deeds have not been forgotten;
Their wealth will remain with their descendants,
And their inheritance with their children's children."
(Sirach 44:1,8,10-12).

God's Love and Fear of Death

*It's not that I'm afraid to die, I just don't want to
be there when it happens.* -Woody Allen

When we are in touch with God's vast love, our fear of death wanes. According to comedian Jerry Seinfeld, people's number one fear is public speaking. Somehow this ranked even higher than fear of death; which means people would rather be in the coffin at a funeral than give a speech.

Another of my favorite jokes about death is, "I sure will be glad when scientists discover a cure for 'Natural Causes'." Then there is the message on the tombstone of the hypochondriac: "I was right!"

Actually there is a lighter side to dying and there are reasons we should not fear death. Every day of the year,

61

365 times, we could read from the bible "Do not be afraid", and not read the same passage twice.

One of my favourites is Isaiah 41:10 "Do not fear, for I am with you." The coming of Jesus brought joy in other ways: "And the angel said unto them, 'Be not afraid; for behold, I bring you good tidings of great joy which shall be to all the people'." (Luke 2:10). A Saviour was born for us.

And my all-time favourite passage underscores this: "Do not be afraid, for I have redeemed you." (Isaiah 43:1). This is followed immediately by "I have called you by your name. You are mine."

"Before I formed you in the womb, I knew you." (Jeremiah 1:5). The thought of my mother and father is a great consolation as I age and approach death. Our forefathers and mothers have gone before us with all the faith and trust with which God blesses us. Why would we fear death? Why would we fear that final meeting when Jesus asks, "Well, how was it?"

A wonderful illustration comes to mind from *The Word Among Us*, September 1995: Sister Marie Clare tells us of the life of an aids victim who had nothing going for her and ended up with "everything". Ingrid was a thirty-five-year-old South African when she arrived at Shepherd's Dwelling. She had full blown aids, complicated by toxoplasmosis which attacks tissues and the nervous system. She also had herpes.

When she arrived, Ingrid told Sister Claire that she did not like God. During her stay at the hospice Ingrid noticed Sister Claire's devoted commitment to daily Mass and started asking questions. Ingrid was touched by the loving care she received. At one point she called her friends together to celebrate and express a "thank you" to them. It was about this time that Ingrid had a dream:

She dreamt that Jesus came to her, lifted her out of her bed, put her on his lap and told her how much he loved her. Ingrid said that Mary was also there with two angels. After a while Jesus told her she had to go back to earth for a bit longer. He put her back into the bed.

Near to the end, Ingrid asked Sister Claire for paper and pencil to write a note for each of her children:

> My Dear Child
> I'm lying here thinking about you – thinking of what I should write. I brought you into this world and have watched you grow up to become a nice young person. I am very proud of you.
> I love you very much and will miss you with all my heart. But I think I will be with you in a very special way. God and Mary will always be with you – in your heart – watching you playing and going to school. I will continue to watch over you and be with you in this very special way.
> I hope you will always keep me in your heart and pray for me.
>
> Love
> Mommy

If we could understand God's great love for us, we would indeed have no fear, even of death. If we knew the height and depth, the breadth and width of God's love, fear would disappear. We would have God in us; in our hearts where God longs to be. And with the life of God in us, we would know that death is not the end. God does not die.

At his installation as Archbishop in Regina October 14, 2016, Most Reverend Donald Bolen reflected on Ephesians 3:17-19 which describes Paul's prayer that through the Spirit we would come to know the breadth and the length, the height and the depth of God's love.

Bolen went on to explain that in Saskatchewan we have a chance to experience the expanse of God's creation. When we see the distant horizon surrounding us we have a sense of vastness.

Now picture the sky at night and see the endlessness of space created by God. We are a mere blue dot in this creation, a dot we have seen from space with our cameras. Now we are closer to seeing the height and the depth, the breadth and the length of the wonderful world God created for us.

Now imagine God's love for us. "Before I formed you in the womb, I knew you … I have loved you with an everlasting love." (Jeremiah 1:5, 31:3). Now think of our place in the thousands of years of salvation history. God has put us here for a purpose.

We carry God's love in us, and through the Resurrection of Jesus we carry God's life in us for eternity. We are challenged to present the breadth and the length, the height and the depth of God's love to the world. If we can do this then the fear of death will disappear. The Resurrection of Christ has defeated death. It is our resurrection as well, and St Paul points out that death has lost its sting: "Death, where is your victory? Death, where is your sting?" (1 Corinthians 15:55).

Jesus said: "I am the resurrection and the life. Whoever believes in me, though he die, yet shall he live."

(John 11:25).

It's A Wonderful Life

The 1946 movie *It's a Wonderful Life,* based on the short story "The Greatest Gift" by Philip Van Doren Stern, is reminiscent of the great literature of Thornton Wilder's *Our Town.* Drama touches the heart on basic questions about temporal and eternal realities.

George Bailey, played by James Stewart, deeply troubled and contemplating suicide, pronounces that he wishes he had never been born. Disaster is averted when the prayers of his family and friends reach heaven. An angel sets out to save George and makes true his wish about never being born.

In this confusing reality change, George sees how different the world would be if he had never touched the lives of his family, friends and neighbours. For example, a war hero who saves his men and is awarded a medal does not exist because George was not there to save him from drowning in childhood. So the men die. Small and large, our impact on those around us is profound. Another example is George's wife who ends up a spinster librarian. Their wonderful family does not exist. Then there is George's business venture the Building and Loan that is endangered when $8,000 gets misplaced. Well, it's a wonderful story which I don't want to spoil.

In the end the angel that saved George gets his wings, and George goes back to his wonderful life. Truth and value survive and are as simply defined as black and white, like this movie, which came out in 1946 and still survives today.

And you and I, after drying our tears, are left with a deep gratitude for life, family, love and spiritual truths. Now what should we do with all this gratitude and profound understanding?

> *A man goes to see a psychiatrist and says, "Doctor, I've got a split personality and it's interfering with my life. It's wrecking my job so I can't get along with...It's ruining my family life. I ... It's destroying my social life..."*
>
> *"Hold it," the doctor shouted. "Now one at a time please."*

Yes, we should be babbling about the wonderful life of Christ we are heir to. When we stop to reflect long enough, we realize that this is a wonderful life. Joy should overwhelm us. There is a quiet dignity to our everyday tasks. These are simple things our parents and grandparents did before us that made up the salvation in their lives. The fabric of our everyday lives makes up our spiritual journey.

Thomas Merton wrote: "It is enough to be, in the ordinary human mode, with one's hunger and sleep, one's cold and warmth, rising and going to bed. Putting on blankets and taking them off, making coffee and drinking it. Defrosting the refrigerator, reading, meditating, working, praying. I live as my fathers have lived on this earth; eventually I die. Amen."

And we have a mission in life. Whether we know it or not, God has given us a key role as His Kingdom unfolds. "Simply by being who you are, you are changing history. Your words, your actions, your demeanor are helping to shape other people and their perception of the Lord. Even your prayers are changing the world." (from *The Word Among Us* October 2014).

Do not let humility hold you back:

"Who am I to bring the people of Israel out of Egypt?" Moses asks. God responds, "You may not be anyone, but I am." (Jason Simon from *The Evangelical Catholic*).

An old adage says, it's not the things you *do* in life that you regret—it's the things you *don't* do. In a paper entitled "The Ideal Road Not Taken," Cornell psychologist researchers found that, when asked to name their single biggest regret in life, 76 percent of participants said they didn't fulfill their *ideal* self. "When it comes to your dreams and aspirations, people are more likely to let them just drift by unrealized, and that's what really stings later in life," the Cornell study says.

"God doesn't require us to succeed, he only requires that we try," St Teresa of Calcutta said.

I am reminded of a scene in John 6:22 where Jesus goes for a walk on the Sea of Galilee. It seems almost out of character that Jesus steps out of natural time, in a sense. I sometimes imagine that He was looking for us out there. Thinking of us.

God is Love. Love is patient; love is kind; love never fades. Faith and Hope and Love abide, but the greatest of these is LOVE. It is best for us to remember this when troubles beset us, and hope fades, when our world is rocked by sorrow and sadness that have us grasping for faith and meaning. Remember then that God is Love.

Chapter 7 Experiencing Loss

Covid-19 has changed our traditional way of handling loss of a loved one. Funerals have been modified or in some cases postponed. The support of family and friends has been limited as memorial gatherings are restricted in number and character. This complicates the processes of grieving discussed in the next four chapters of this book.

Grieving is a complicated and individual process. The chapters that follow will address general principles that apply to coping with loss and concentrate on the comfort and solace faith and God's love can provide.

I repeat, when our world is rocked by sorrow and sadness that have us grasping for faith and meaning, remember then that God is Love.

When a Loved One Dies

"The mercury sank in the mouth of the dying day.

O all the instruments agree
The day of his death was a dark cold day."
("In Memory of W.B. Yeats" W.H. Auden)

I was summoned from the classroom in Radisson High School just before noon. The call had gone out to family members that it was now a matter of hours. I gathered my things, leaving instructions which had been prepared days ahead of this, and raced from the school. I headed toward the highway losing no time on the winter ice.

Just before the railway tracks a car stopped in from of me. I braked, and braked, and kept pumping the brake. Finally, in desperation I put my foot down and held it there, uttering a prayer. I stopped perhaps an inch from his bumper.

I took a deep breath and relaxed a little. I had been making this trip home to Saskatoon for weeks now, always racing back to St Paul's Hospital after school to see how my father was before heading back to our apartment where my wife was busy with her studies and supper.

Every mile inched by as I recalled Dylan Thomas's words, "Do not go gentle into that good night / Rage, rage against the dying of the light." "Wise men" know that their end is right, but "they do not go gentle into that good night".

My father "cursed me", "blessed me" with his struggle. He said he would fight until the last dog was hung! His "fierce tears" blessed me now. It is natural and right to fight that good fight to the last breath, even as it is right to trust in God to deliver you in that hour.

My father's death in December 1970 was not my first experience with death, but he was the first member of our immediate family to die. Death was always something that happened to others, not to us. We were the survivors as we left the graveyard after each funeral. That all changed when one of us remained.

The earth has been cut deeply
Like an open wound
Through my heart
There is nothing to do
But to stop

Tomorrow I will reboot the main frame
And the day after
I will continue until the scar is less sore
Until I can go on

Someone you love has just died. Now what? When separation from a loved one occurs, there is little one can say to take away the pain. One leading theologian said, "We need to put our mouths to the dust and wait for time and God to heal us." Friends and family can support us, often in silence.

Our first thought should be *Resurrection*. I have gone through enough Easter celebrations to realize that what follows the Good Friday suffering and death is glorious Resurrection. After losing four parents, six siblings and many uncles, aunts and my grandparents, the theme of Resurrection brings me tremendous consolation when death takes a close family member.

When my father died, I felt numb. The Funeral Prayers and Funeral Mass were endured in a state of controlled sorrow. But consolation came in time. After losing my parents and parent in laws, over time and with

70

God's Grace, I have come to accept the many consolations that come with loss. Faith assures us of that banquet of heaven where there is no suffering and where there are no tears. "With thoughts like these you should console one another." (1 Thessalonians 4:18).

After absorbing losses through the years, I have come to the point where when I left the hospital following my father-in-law's death, I sang alleluias through my tears. Later, when my mother-in-law was born to eternal life, I left the hospital singing one of her favorite songs, "I was full of Joy, alleluia, when I set out for the house of the Lord." Still there were tears. That's natural.

It is never easy, accepting that final blow. I was with my brother when his doctor shared the news of his terminal cancer. I was in some degree of shock as I left my brother in the loving arms of his family, and I drove back home for three and a half hours listening to Jesse Cook's *Narada* and *Free Fall* and reminiscing childhood memories of growing up with my brother on the family farm. After three hours I felt better. Both feet were back on the ground.

I have not experienced the loss of a spouse. Nothing can prepare you for that, but with age and experience you are not left empty handed. There are adaptability tools you can have in your arsenal for that eventuality. There is a powerful metaphor that expresses our ability to stand against grief with the power of faith. Carleen Gerber, First Congregational Church, relates this story about her father called "The Anchor Holds":

> When I was a child my dad was a
> seasoned sailor .... I remember quite
> clearly a time when a squall came up in

the night, and our anchor dragged. With thunder and lightening flashing around us, and the rain pelting the decks and limiting our visibility, our boat went drifting very slowly but steadily toward the shore.

My father started up the engines and then stood very calmly "at the ready," keeping watch. He knew that the anchor was large, and he hoped that the anchor would catch hold of something new and strong on the bottom, before we hit the shore. And that the engines would be unnecessary.

The flukes on this anchor drop down into the mud or the rocks at the sand at the bottom of the sea. As the boat pulls with all its weight against this main shaft of the anchor, the flukes drive themselves further into the soil. An anchor weighing 20 to 25 pounds could hold a boat weighing several tons, once the anchor sets well into the mud.

We dragged, slowly, quite a long way. But eventually, the anchor caught hold. And you could feel the whole boat pull herself taut against the anchor line and right herself into the wind of the storm.

The story of the boat dragging anchor in a squall is a good metaphor for the process of grief. The storm of grief tends to make us feel as if we are helplessly tossed about by waves and wind. It can destabilise us and make us feel as if we don't know what the future holds. It can erode our self-confidence.

Those who want most to help us are best advised to keep watch nearby. Their patience and calm and love are far more important than their skills. And there is, for the most part, nothing anyone can do to lessen our grief.

But our faith, I believe, is like that anchor. It's hard to see it, clearly, way down there at the bottom. And it's hard to trust that something so small can be effective against a storm that rages and a boat that is so heavy. But our faith does hold us in the storm. We can trust the anchor. We can trust our faith.

Let me share a distinction between grieving and mourning that Doctor Alan Wolfelt presents: "*Grief* is what we think and feel on the inside when we lose someone or something important. ... *Mourning* is the word for grief expressed. While grief is what's bottled up inside you, mourning is the opening up, the letting out, and the sharing."

Without mourning, grief festers, Wolfelt says. Grief does not go away with time alone. If it is expressed honestly, through mourning, many ongoing problems like depression, anxiety, substance abuse and others can be avoided. Mourning can open us up to a life that is again rewarding and rich.

What wonderful news that mourning can actually free us to experience life more fully and deeply. Sorrow enriches us with healing memories. How balanced it all seems after the healing provided by mourning and years of remembering a loved one. Yet how raw and painful and numbing is the initial grief or loss felt by death's absolute separation. The more deeply our love for someone, the more painful the loss of separation.

Chapter 8 will discuss aspects of grief that may help us understand our personal encounters with loss. We can apply Dr Bill Webster's healing strategies to our individual experiences and know that we are normal, that how we express our grief is natural.

Chapter 8 Healing Strategies of Grief

A Guest Article written by Dr Bill Webster

We live in a culture that often denies or avoids the subjects of death and significant loss. The same factors that affect our attitude towards death influence and even aggravate society's perception of **grief**, which is often minimised, misunderstood and unmentioned.

People seem reluctant to recognise the painful process of grief. The messages they give the grieving person are conflicting. Things like *"you must be strong; pull yourself together; you mustn't cry; life must go on"*, suggest that grief is unnecessary and even unacceptable. We haven't learned what *is* normal and what we can expect after a significant loss.

When people find themselves unavoidably confronted with loss and struggling with grief, it can be one of the most difficult experiences of life. Yet at the very time when they may most need support from friends and family, many are confronted by a conspiracy of silence around this whole subject of grief.

There is a real need for us to first and foremost understand and legitimise the long-term process of grief and to validate the many emotions and reactions that can affect someone after a loss. Grief may be a natural reaction to loss, yet saying it is normal does not minimise its difficulty. Grief is one of life's most challenging experiences, and often we need help to come to terms with it.

Much has been written on the subject of grief, and many different authors have their own "system" to explain the process, and frankly I have found many to be insightful and helpful, albeit different. Because grief is such a unique experience to each individual, *there is no one formula or description* that embraces all aspects of the experience. Every group and every individual experience is different, and just when you think you've heard it all, someone tells you ***their*** story and opens up a whole new area of understanding and insight.

My book **"When Someone You Care about Dies"** gives the grieving person something of an insight to the grief process, and many groups use it as a work book in their sessions. It is deliberately short and to the point, which many grieving people have told me is exactly what they need.

## 1.	What is Grief?

Dr Therese Rando describes grief as ***"the process of psychological, social and somatic reactions to the perception of loss."*** Dr Alan Wolfelt describes grief as ***"an emotional suffering caused by a death or another form of bereavement."*** Dr Wolfelt makes the distinction between grief and mourning, describing grief as "the internal meaning given to the external event", while mourning is "the outward expression of grief". Bereavement, incidentally, is usually defined as "the state of having suffered a loss", the root word "reave" literally meaning "to be torn apart".

The definition that I have found most practical, if

76

less clinical, in working with grief support groups is:

"Grief is a natural reaction, often manifesting itself in a bewildering cluster of ordinary human emotions in response to any significant loss, intensified and complicated by the relationship lost."

This definition allows us to understand the grief experience in several ways.

a)   Grief is an Unwelcome Experience:

While loss is inevitable in this life, no-one welcomes the experience. When people are grieving, they are reacting to the fact that they have had a loss; someone they care about has died; they are acknowledging that they need some help through this experience, which is probably much more difficult, emotional and long lasting than they had ever anticipated, even though many around them may be telling them to "get over it". All of these things are enormously difficult to acknowledge, far less cope with.

b)   Grief is a Natural Human Experience:

Our definition affirms my strong, unshakable conviction that grief is a normal reaction to an unwelcome event. Grief is not a sickness or a disease. It is the normal, human response to a significant loss. While there may be pathological or complicated elements that grief can generate, the reaction to a significant loss is a natural reaction. People may be encouraged to "be strong" or "not to cry". But how sad it would be if someone we cared about died and we didn't cry, or we carried on as if nothing had happened. Frankly, I'd like to think that someone would miss me enough to shed a tear after I'm gone. Wouldn't you?

When you lose someone special from your life you are going to grieve. Our grief is saying that we miss the person and that we're struggling to adjust to a life without that special relationship. Admittedly, saying that grief is *normal* does not minimise its ***difficulty***. That is why I lean more to using the word "natural" rather than "normal". Grief may be one of the most challenging experiences of life. But the person experiencing it is not crazy, or weak, or "not handling things". They are experiencing grief, and after a significant loss, that is a natural response.

What we do by educating people in this way is to VALIDATE the experience of grief. *Validating the significance of grief and legitimising the albeit difficult process is the greatest gift we can give to any grieving person.* When you have legitimised the process, people are free to then "work through" their grief issues. They know they are not crazy. They realise that their grief is not a reflection on their coping skills; grief is an indication that they CARED. Thus liberated from the stigma of grief, which is that "you ought to be doing better, or be 'over it'", they can begin the grief journey of exploring their feelings and making the adjustments they need to make.

Sometimes people ask me "What is the worst kind of loss?" Is it worse to lose a spouse or to lose a child? Others question if it is worse to lose someone after a long lingering illness, or if they die suddenly and unexpectedly from a heart attack or in an accident. On one hand there is no answer to such a question. Perhaps the best response is to affirm, ***"The worst kind of loss is yours***." A loss is a very personal matter. Your loss seems like the worst possible thing that could have happened to you. While these circumstances make each loss different, they are not important right now. The worst kind of grief is *yours*. When you lose a significant person from your life, whatever the relationship, it hurts, and nothing takes away from your right to feel the loss and grieve the absence of that person from your life.

c)   Grief is a Uniquely Personal Experience:

Every individual is unique. We are all different, in looks, in character, in cultural diversity, as well as in human experiences. People vary in gender, age, family background, and personal loss histories. The relationship they lost was unique. Not only is it important to differentiate the loss of spouse with the loss of a child, parent, sibling, family member or friend, all of which have their own unique stresses and challenges; it is also vital to recognise that even within these broad categories there are many different situations. Every marriage is unique: some are longer lasting, more interactive, happier than are others. Every relationship is unique and the legal definition is just the beginning of the diversity.

My relationship with my parents will not be the same as yours has been. So if both of us lose our fathers, why should we expect that our grief reaction should be similar, just because our losses are alike? You are a unique person, as am I. Our fathers were different people. The relationships we shared with our fathers were distinctive. And probably the circumstances surrounding the individual deaths would be quite separate. And the same goes for a spouse and all other relationships.

Why then does society seem to expect every person in every situation to grieve in exactly the same way? ***If you are looking for a cookie cutter formula by which to offer support, same thing for every individual and situation, then you've got the wrong book!*** Every grief is unique. That's what makes this work so exciting. While there may be many similarities, every individual manifests grief in a way that is appropriate for them, and that is affected and moulded by such variables as gender, family history, cultural context, loss history, beliefs and values, the age of deceased and griever, mode of death whether anticipated or sudden, and availability and *perceived* appropriateness of support, as well as a full understanding of the relationship lost and what that means to the individual.

d)   Grief is an Emotional Experience:

Grief is an emotional response to a significant loss. Because it is an emotion, it is difficult to describe. The Scots have a saying that some things are better "felt than tell't" (tell it). Grief is one of these things. Whenever we lose someone (or something), or an attachment is broken, we can experience a painful reaction. To experience grief is to acknowledge that you have loved someone, and now that person has gone. If you hadn't needed that relationship, or risked the emotional attachment, you wouldn't be feeling the loss. But you did, and, oh yes, it was worth the risk. It is a high compliment to any relationship that we miss it enough to shed a tear and feel emotional. How awful if we didn't! Tears are not a sign of weakness, but an indication of how special the relationship was. And, now that it is gone, we miss it. To experience grief is to acknowledge that you are human.

Because we have not understood grief, its intensity often comes as a surprise. We can find ourselves bewildered by the avalanche of emotions that can impact us. Among these emotions are numbness, shock, confusion, disbelief, anxiety, absent-mindedness, restlessness, crying, fatigue, appetite disorders, sleep disruptions, physical symptoms, anger, guilt, depression, and many more. What other emotions can YOU think of that can be connected to grief?

Just as every individual is unique, so every person's grief process is unique. This somehow comes as a surprise to many. Some people experience certain emotions, other people experience others. Everyone is different, and so the way you respond to your unique loss will not be the same as anyone else's. That is why the word "cluster" seems so appropriate in the definition.

One of my weaknesses in life is a love of chocolate, particularly nut clusters. After a lifetime of research, I have made an amazing discovery. There are no two nut clusters exactly the same! While each consists of the same basic ingredients, every single one is different. Some are round while others are a little "off shape", some containing a few extra nuts, others have a bigger blob of chocolate on top. Same ingredients, yet none are identical.

Similarly, grief is a cluster of emotions. Make a list of some of these emotions that YOU have experienced.

Yet we all have our own unique cluster, just because we are all different people. One person may experience many of the emotions of grief, but always to a lesser or greater degree than someone else.

That's why I *never* say, "I know how you feel." I don't! How can I? All I know is how I felt when grief touched my life. Just because one person experiences something one way does not mean another person is abnormal because their experience is different. Yet it is amazing how many people do not give others the freedom to grieve in a way that is right for them. Everyone is unique. Their situation and the relationship they have lost is unique. So do not be surprised if their response to their loss is unique, and especially if they do not live up to *your* expectations of what is an appropriate response. There is a reason for every reaction, and if we care to find out what that is, it will be insightful.

e) Grief is a Painful Experience:

Part of our culture's death denying posture is evidenced in how we tend to move away from pain. We can often distance ourselves from it, sometimes going to great lengths to shield ourselves from things that are unpleasant. Take for example the fact that the vast majority of individuals no longer die in their homes. Death is more likely to occur in a nursing home or hospital, sometimes, sadly, away from his or her own familiar surroundings, family and friends. While this may mean that family members need not be made to feel uncomfortable by watching someone they love die, it can sometimes be an avoidance behaviour.

Yet, grief is painful. It hurts to lose anyone we care about. Loss is one of the most difficult human challenges, and there is no easy way around it. People may try to avoid the pain, and others may attempt to get the individual "over it" as quickly as possible. But most of the time it simply doesn't work that way. All that attitude accomplishes is to isolate the grieving individual, who feels they can't share their true feelings with anyone, and who cries alone at night, all the while feeling they are "not handling it".

The way out of grief is **through** it. As Helen Keller says, "The only way to get to the other side is to go through the door." As we validate the grief experience, people come to realise that pain is a gift that warns us of danger. It can actually be a sign of healing, as we make the painful adjustments from life before the death to life after the death. It is this that enables us to reorganise, to learn, to grow. People need to find the courage to go through the painful experience of grief, and helpers need to find ways to enable them to move into and through the pain. This is one of the keys to recovery.

f)   Grief is a Manageable Experience:

It is never too early in the process to sow seeds of hope. Hope that the grieving individual will make it through the process. They will be given confidence when you can impart to them that they are not abnormal or unusual. Rather you see them as good people who have been temporarily overwhelmed by their situation and who with help and support will be able to make it through this difficult time.

While many friends are supportive around the time of the death, grieving people often discover that support fades shortly after the funeral. When someone is going through a bad time, people tend to leave them alone, often because the situation makes THEM feel uncomfortable. We aren't quite sure what to say or do, and many end up saying and doing nothing. I know many grieving people who feel quite abandoned after their loss, even though this is not the intention of their friends.

After a loss, people need to talk. To be more accurate, they need to talk and talk and talk, sometimes repeating the same story over and over. Part of the resolution of grief is found in reviewing the events of the person's life and death and reliving their memories. Because of the isolationist society we have previously described, many do not feel they can share with friends or even family. This is why I believe there has been such an increase in grief support groups. The opportunity to share with others of similar experience can help bring resolution.

Yet it is always a struggle. Grief is difficult. It is never easy to lose someone or something you have relied on. This is possibly the most difficult experience of life. Some people, after a loss, see themselves as victims. They refuse to struggle to come to terms with the situation. But as we struggle, we discover that in every loss there is a gain. There will be times when the grieving person will wonder if they can make it, but your involvement will help them to find the confidence that they can. Little by little you will help them discover strength and resources they you didn't know they had.

Expectant mothers have labour pains, teenagers have growing pains, butterflies struggle to come out of their cocoon, but out of that struggle and that pain comes growth and life. Life is never without struggle, but it is out of that very struggle that we find strength. That doesn't make the pain any easier, but it does help put it in a meaningful context.

Chapter 9

Children and Grieving
And

When You Lose a Child

"Earth hath no sorrow that heaven
cannot heal." -St Thomas More

When I was a child my first cousin was killed in an accident. The fear of death became real to me. Death lurked in the dark only feet away. I knew about God and angels and the spiritual world, but now I also knew about death. Having family close by was terribly important to me. The thought that you could lose a family member was disconcerting. Thoughts of my own mortality were terrifying.

Sometimes adults deal with the grief of loss by sending the children to be with a relative so that the adults can make the necessary arrangements and handle the emotional trauma that overwhelms them. That is a mistake. Children need the close family ties and support at this crucial time.

In *Roses in December* Marilyn Willet Heavilin shares the story of losing her baby by crib death. Her daughter shared the same room. As the adults focused on the dead child, his sister, who was three, huddled against the wall on her bed. When they finally noticed her first words were, "I didn't hurt Jimmy."

After mom's quick assurance that she had done no wrong and that an angel had taken Jimmy to heaven to be with Jesus, her daughter was visibly relieved. Later Heavilin's daughter visited her during the night and was moving her hand across her mom's face. "I just wanted to see if God took you too," she explained. The three-year-old reverted to baby talk and babyish mannerisms. It took two or three years before Heavilin's daughter became the relaxed and carefree girl she had been.

A pamphlet distributed by Mothers Against Drunk Driving (MADD) outlines how children of certain ages cope with the reality of death:

> A child of two can sense loss and suffer the feelings that go with loss, but cannot understand what death is. The child will pick up on the grief and anxiety in his surroundings and will need touching or holding. Explanations, however, will not be understood. The child this young can only understand that someone is present or not present.
>
> What one does is far more important to the child this young than what one says. Generally, it is best done with large doses of tender loving care — holding, cuddling, and stroking.
>
> A child between the ages of four to six may talk of the death of the person in the same detached way that he may talk of the death of a pet. This may be disturbing to the adults around him, and their reaction may be confusing. Crying may be more out of confusion about what others are experiencing rather than the death itself.
>
> Most commonly, seven or eight-year-olds become fearful of death because they realize for the first time that it is real … Some of their questions may indicate fears

of their own death. Death can now be seen as an attacker who takes life. Although able to accept the finality of death, many of the factors of early childhood still apply. It is important for children of this age to express their sadness, anger, fear, and guilt.

(Janice C. Harris and Angela Bennet, "Helping Children Cope with Death in the Family". Hurst, Texas: *Mothers Against Drunk Drivers*, 1984, pamphlet).

In *Roses in December* Heavilin shares some of her experiences with mourning. When she was twelve, her uncle and aunt were fatally injured in a gas stove explosion. Her parents wanted to leave her with a babysitter while they drove to the hospital. Heavilin insisted on going along. Later she sat with her grandmother as the news of her uncle's death was delivered. Next morning she was at the hospital as her aunt passed away. The family was going to see her aunt's children and Heavilin wanted to accompany them. The doctor said she could not go. She cried, "Are they dying, too?" Her mother realized the situation and insisted she be allowed to see her cousins.

During the week of the funeral Heavilin recalls that few adults spoke with her. When she returned to school her teacher came up to her, put her arms around her and asked her how she was doing. The tears flooded her eyes and she sobbed while her teacher held her.

It is important that we realize that death affects children too, and not just their parents. Seek out children and ask them how they are doing. If they don't want to talk, that is fine. Play a game or share some other activity with them. Help preserve their feelings of self-worth Heavilin suggests.

91

Teenagers can have a very difficult time with the loss of someone close to them. I remember the death of a friend in high school that affected us all deeply. For days we lived in shock while our friend lost his struggle for life. It was very important to congregate with other teens and give each other support.

Teens are often more empathetic than some adults. Heavilin shares her experience with the loss of her teen son Nathan who was killed by a drunk driver. One of her students sent her a note on the first-year anniversary of Nate's death:

> I just wanted you to know that I was thinking about you today. I know this must be a difficult time for you. Nathan was very special to all of us, and even though I miss him greatly, I'm sure I can't begin to understand the depths of your love for him and the mixed emotions you must have at this time. I only pray that God will continue to comfort you with the awesome fact that Nathan beat the rest of us home! Andy

When You Lose a Child

Unnatural and heart-wrenching may describe the loss of a child. Then there is the shock.

In *Angel Girl* author Father Craig Harrison gives us a resource for children who are suffering and a resource for their friends and family. *Angel Girl* helps deal with the reality of death and the afterlife. *Angel Girl* breathes the words of eleven-year-old Lauren Small, and shares with readers how her life was really part of God's plan for her to be an Angel Girl.

In the book God is addressing countless unborn children, explaining the contest He is going to have. The girl who can teach love to everyone around her will be crowned Angel Girl. When young Lauren gets sick, she sets out to share love with her doctors, nurses, and fellow patients. *Angel Girl* invites readers to share love as Lauren does. Obedience to God and trust in his plan reassures us, just as it carried Lauren through two years of cancer treatment to the new life God plans for all of us.

Coping with Miscarriage

If you have experienced the loss of a child or had a miscarriage, what do you wish other people would understand about it?

Losing a child is a particularly difficult experience. No one is prepared for that painful reality. Malka Ahmed shares these thoughts on line:

"Six Things I Wish People Knew About Grieving the Loss of a Child"
October 26, 2015 by Malka Ahmed

One: Grief and Love are the same.
Please don't think that because I am still grieving for my child even after all this time that there is something wrong with me, or that I need to get over it. I grieve deeply for the loss of my child because I also love

her deeply. Love never dies, therefore neither will grief.

Two: I will never get over it.

I may look like I finally got my life back together. I may have even gone on to have more children or embarked on a new career, but my child and the trauma of losing her is always one step behind. My tears may have dried, and I can probably utter my child's name without breaking apart, but please know that I will never, ever get over the fact that she is gone.

Three: Silence is deafening.

I know it must be very difficult and confusing to know what to say to someone who has lost a child. I know how uncomfortable and unfathomable it must be to you, but please know that wrongly worded sentiments are easier to forgive than your silence. My world has forever been shattered; a simple "I'm sorry" will do.

Four: My child is irreplaceable.

It doesn't matter when my loss may have occurred, whether it was an early miscarriage, or if I had the chance to spend a few moments with my child before she died. Babies are not interchangeable and any subsequent child born after is not a replacement.

Five: I'll always live in a parallel universe.

No matter how much time has gone by, when an important holiday or occasion occurs, my mind is going to retreat into another universe where my child would have been present. I will calculate how old they would be and how they would look.

Six: I am forever changed.

The day my child died is the same day a big part of me died too. I won't go back to being my usual innocent and carefree self again. It will take time for me to find myself, and return back home. But when I've figured out a way to put together all the broken pieces, I won't look the same. Please understand that.

Children, Angels and Grieving

One of the most difficult aspects of the loss of a loved one has to do with helping children with the grieving process. As a grandfather I have been part of this process and wish to share my experience with my readers.

Ideally the burden is lightened where faith exists in the family. Children can be closer to God than we often expect. Take for example when I was assisting my grandchildren while their mother was in hospital after giving birth by way of a C-section. I noticed the two girls stopping during their play and kneeling to say a prayer for mommy and the baby. God has a great love for each of us, and we are like a family to him. When children get to know this, then explaining God's will to them becomes easier.

When my son-in-law's father was born to eternal life, I sent a communication to my grandchildren to help them cope with the loss. This is the content of that letter from Grandpa Ken.

Grandpas know about Angels

When I was a little boy before I went to school, I was playing near a deep washout caused by years of spring run-off through a ravine that wound for several miles. The flowing water was irresistible, and I, a child in rubber boots, was perched on a huge rock right at the edge where the water roared into the washout. I slipped and plunged into the water. I was out so quickly I am still not sure how. It is as if a huge hand reached in and pulled me out.

Later I found out about how angels look after us. God has given each of us a guardian angel who is with us all the time.

There are true stories told about these angels. I want to share two of them with you. A boy who almost died from a ruptured appendix tells us he met his great grandfather in heaven.

When Colton Burpo from Nebraska was four years old he was on a trip to Colorado. He got very sick and had to undergo emergency surgery twice. As he lay on the operating table, Colton, now eleven, says he went to heaven. *Heaven Is For Real,* a book of his experience, has since become a New York Times Best Seller.

Colten said he didn't recognise "Pop", the family's nick name for their great grand father, from a picture taken shortly before his death, but from one of him as a young man. Colton told his astonished parents that he had met the sister his mother had miscarried a year before his own birth. Colton also described to his astonished parents how he had seen them praying for him.

Colton's dad Todd said: "At first we were surprised. What grabbed my attention was that he could tell me where I was praying - my own wife couldn't tell me that."

Speaking last month about the sister he never knew he had, Colten said: "She looked familiar and she started giving me hugs and told me she was glad to have someone from her family up there. She doesn't have a name though, she said they never gave her one. But she can't wait for her mom and dad to come to Heaven to meet her."

He went on to recount heaven in more detail, saying: "I remember Jesus. There's streets of gold and a lot of colours. I sat on Jesus' lap and then I just felt safe. God, he is the biggest one in Heaven, he can hold the world in his hands."

When asked what Heaven is like, Colton said: "Well, it's all the colours of the rainbow, a place of beautiful shades and hues. The gates were made of gold and there were pearls on them. It never gets dark. It's always bright. Everyone has wings and can fly except for Jesus, who hovers up and down. Everyone wears a white robe crossed by a sash of different colours and they have lights above their heads."

Colton said publishing the book was not something he intended to do, but he said he again turned to God for an answer. He prayed: "God, if this is really you. I don't know how to publish a book. If you want me to do this you will have the publishing industry come to me." And they did. Mr Burpo, a garage-door salesman and a minister said: "I don't know why He picked us. God did a remarkable miracle for us."

The second story I want to share with you is about angels. In a book called *Angels on Earth, May/June 2001,* there is a story of a young North Carolina girl named Deb who tells her Grandmother about a dream she had. "Last night I dreamed about Grandpa," she says. When Deb relates how she saw Grandpa slip into a green robe, her Grandmother's eyes fill with tears. "He made it, Deb," she says. "He really made it."

Grandma goes on to say, "One Sunday at church…grandpa saw an angel standing on the altar…at least ten feet tall…wearing the most beautiful green robe… 'When I get to heaven,' he said, 'I want a green robe just like the one that angel was wearing'".

Jesus told us that children have angels who look after them (Matthew 18:10), and these angels are also with God.

YOUR GRANDPA has gone to be with God and the angels. God saw that Grandpa was suffering and took him home to heaven. Heaven is the place where there is no sickness, no pain and no suffering.

God loves us so much that he often sends us signs and messages to make our lives better.

When Jesus lived on earth he looked after his friends. When it was time, Jesus told them that he was going to go to heaven, but that he would still look after them.

Your Grandpa has gone to heaven, but now he can look after us and be near us everyday. Grandpa is an angel now and still loves us very much. You can pray to Grandpa to ask God to look after Grandma or your mom and dad. And Grandpa can talk to God.

You have other family members who are with God and you can talk to them too, like Great Grandpa George or your little brother who went to heaven before he was born.

Your Grandpa died and went to heaven on Saturday,

the day before Ascension Sunday. Ascension Sunday is the day Jesus went to heaven. On that day people all over the world celebrated happily that Jesus has gone to heaven where he can be close to God and help to look after us.

That is Grandpa's job now. He is close to God and we can talk to him to ask God to help us with anything. Like if we are not feeling well, we can ask to get better. We can ask Grandpa to help look after Grandma and our other family members and friends.

I have asked Grandpa to look after you and to help you not to be too sad. We need to be happy for Grandpa because he is strong again and can move around again without any pain.

If you had a race with Grandpa now, he could beat you.

I love you guys very much. Help mommy and daddy to be happy that Grandpa is in heaven now.

Love,
Grandpa Ken

We have gone through several chapters dealing with fear of death, the process of dying and healing strategies after loss. There remains a key piece to the process of grieving and healing after loss and that is the chapter on Suicide and the devastating effect it can have on us.

Given the statistics on Covid-19's impact on suicide numbers, a deeper understanding and a theology of suicide are a must.

Chapter 10
Suicide and Theology of Suicide

The hibiscus flower, unusually beautiful, stays but a single day and then is gone forever. The health and beauty of our body blooms so briefly, sometimes unnoticed. God notices and marks the event in the great book. Without every hibiscus flower that ever gave up its beauty, the world would be slightly less beautiful. The death of a flower reminds us that each day of bloom is infinitely better than an eternity of plastic. And so, suicide victims die. We look on and spill real tears, over real life and real beauty that, however transitory, has left a lasting impact on God's creation.

(Metaphor borrowed from *Against an Infinite Horizon* by Ron Rolheiser O.M.I.)

Introduction

Every year theologian and author Father Ron Rolheiser publishes an article on suicide in almost 100 newspapers in North American and around the world. I will share (with permission) one of these articles as an immediate consolation for those wounded by suicide:

Suicide: When Someone Is Too Bruised

To Be Touched – by Father Ron Rolheiser

A few days ago, I was asked to visit a family who had, just that day, lost their 19-year-old son to suicide. There isn't much one can offer by way of consolation, even faith consolation, at a moment like this, when everyone is in shock and the pain is so raw.

Few things can so devastate us as the suicide of a loved one, especially of one's own child. There is the horrific shock of losing a loved one so suddenly which, just of itself, can bring us to our knees. But, with suicide, there are other soul-wrenching feelings, too: confusion, guilt, second-guessing, religious anxiety. Where did we fail this person? What might we still have done? What should we have noticed? What is this person's state with God?

What needs to be said about all of this? First of all, that suicide is a disease and the most misunderstood of all sicknesses. It takes a person out of life against his or her will - the emotional equivalent of cancer, a stroke, or a heart attack. Second, we, those left behind, need not spend undue energy second-guessing as to how we might have failed that person, what we should have noticed, and what we might still have done to prevent the suicide.

Suicide is an illness and, as with any sickness, we can love someone and still not be able to save that person from death. God loved this person, too, and, like us, could not, this side of eternity, do anything either.

Finally, we shouldn't worry too much about how God meets this person on the other side. God's love, unlike ours, can go through locked doors and touch what will not allow itself to be touched by us.

Is this making light of suicide? Hardly. Anyone who has ever dealt with either the victim of a suicide before his or her death or with those grieving that death afterward knows that it is impossible to make light of it. There is no hell and there is no pain like the one suicide inflicts. Nobody who is healthy wants to die and nobody who is healthy wants to burden his or her loved ones with this kind of pain.

And that's the point: This is done only when someone isn't healthy. The fact that medication can often prevent suicide should tell us something.

Suicide is an illness -- not a sin. Nobody just calmly decides to commit suicide and burden his or her loved ones with that death any more than anyone calmly decides to die of cancer and cause pain. The victim of suicide (in all but rare cases) is a trapped person, caught up in a fiery, private chaos that has its roots both in his or her emotions and in his or her biochemistry. Suicide is a desperate attempt to end unendurable pain, akin to throwing oneself through a window because one's clothing is on fire.

Many of us have known victims of suicide and we know, too, that in almost every case that person was not full of ego, pride, haughtiness, and the desire to hurt someone. Generally, it's the opposite. The victim has cancerous problems precisely because he or she is wounded, raw, and too bruised to have the necessary resiliency needed to deal with life. Those of us who have lost loved ones to suicide know that the problem is not one of strength but of weakness; the person is too bruised to be touched.

I remember a comment I overheard at a funeral for a suicide victim. The priest had preached badly, hinting that this suicide was somehow the man's own fault and that suicide was always the ultimate act of despair. At the reception afterward a neighbour of the victim expressed his displeasure at the priest's homily: "There are a lot of people in this world who should kill themselves," he lamented bitterly, "but those kind never do! This man is the last person who should have killed himself because he was one of the most sensitive people I've ever met!"

A book could be written on that statement. Too often it is precisely the meek who seem to lose the battle, at least in this world.

Finally, I submit that we shouldn't

worry too much about how God meets our loved ones who have fallen victim to suicide. God, as Jesus assures us, has a special affection for those of us who are too bruised and wounded to be touched. Jesus assures us, too, that God's love can go through locked doors and into broken places and free up what's paralyzed and help that which can no longer help itself. God is not blocked when we are. God can reach through.

And so our loved ones who have fallen victim to suicide are now inside of God's embrace, enjoying a freedom they could never quite enjoy here and being healed through a touch that they could never quite accept from us.

(Oblate Father Ron Rolheiser is a theologian, teacher and award-winning author at the Oblate School of Theology in San Antonio, Texas.)

In a preface to his 2019 article on suicide "Redeeming the Memory of a Loved One" Father Rolheiser shares these thoughts:

One year ago, virtually everyone who knew him was stunned by the suicide death of the most prominent American Hispanic theologian that we have produced up to now, Virgilio Elizondo. Moreover, Virgil wasn't just a very gifted, pioneering theologian, he was also a beloved priest and a warm, trusted friend to countless people. Everyone dies, and the death of a loved one is always hard, but it was the manner of his death that left so many people stunned and confused. Suicide! But he was such a faith-filled, sensitive man. How could this be possible?

And those questions, like the muddy waters of a flood, immediately began to seep into other emotional crevices, leaving most everyone who knew him with a huge, gnawing question: What does this do to his work, to the gift that he left to the church and to the Hispanic community? Can we still honour his life and his contribution in the same way as we would have had he died of a heart attack or cancer? Indeed, had he died of a heart attack or cancer, his death, though sad, would undoubtedly have had about it an air of healthy closure, even of celebration, that we were saying farewell to a great man we had had the privilege to know, as opposed to the air of hush, unhealthy quiet, and unclean grief that permeated the air at his funeral.

Sadly, and this is generally the case when anyone dies by suicide, the manner of that death becomes a prism through which his or her life and work are now seen, coloured, and permanently tainted. It shouldn't be so, and it's incumbent on us, the living who love them, to redeem their memories, to not take their photos off our walls, to not speak in guarded terms about their deaths, and to not let the particular manner of their deaths colour and taint the goodness of their lives. Suicide is the least glamorous and most misunderstood of all deaths. We owe it to our loved ones, and to ourselves, to not further compound a tragedy.

One fear of the surviving members of suicide victim's family is for their eternal salvation. Given the taboo against the act and the commandments of God about the sacredness of life, this is a real concern. Generally this fear is groundless. Death by suicide is against the free will of the victim. We do not freely choose death by heart attack or cancer. We do not fling ourselves into fire or leap from a building unless we are fleeing something more terrible that has taken our reason prisoner.

God's love and compassion goes far beyond ours. Christ can pass through barriers set up by our fears or even death itself. It is even possible for us to bind our loved ones to the family of God even if they have strayed. Theologian Father Ron Rolheiser puts it this way:

> If someone whom you love strays from the church in terms of faith practice and morality, as long as you continue to love that person and hold him or her in love and forgiveness, he or she is touching the "hem of Christ's garment", is being held to the Body of Christ, and is being forgiven by God, irrespective of his or her official external relationship to the church. How?
>
> They are touching the Body of Christ because your touch is Christ's touch. When

you touch someone, unless that person actively rejects your love and forgiveness, he or she is relating to the Body of Christ. And this is true even beyond death: If someone close to you dies in a state which, externally at least, has him or her at odds with the visible church, your love and forgiveness will continue to bind that person to the Body of Christ and will continue to offer forgiveness to that individual, even after death.

Rolheiser goes on to explain: "We are the Body of Christ. What Jesus did for us, we can do for each other. Our love and forgiveness are the cords that connect our loved ones to God, to salvation, and to the community of saints, even when they are no longer walking the path of explicit faith."

Suicide – finding consolation

Death by suicide complicates the normal processes of mourning and loss. Suicide is one of the most devastating ways to lose a loved one. But for the families of suicide victims there is a great consolation based on hope and the absolute certainty of God's love for us.

Here is an example the mother of a suicide victim shared with me that illustrates some of the aspects we want to address in this chapter. (Used with her generous permission)

Hi, my name is Wanda Jackson and I lost my son to suicide Aug. 26, 2008, and today I am feeling really sad. I miss my son very much!!! I found my son hanging in our garage and I cut him down and tried to revive him. Wow, I am so, so tired of going over the tragedy in my head. I have not been to church in six weeks.

I am Apostolic and my pastor is a very kind man. However, a week after my son died I was talking to my pastor and he told me that my son Kevin was separated from God forever. His words crushed me; it was not what I needed to hear from him. I did not ask, so I didn't feel he should have offered this horrible news to me. He talks about suicide more than I've ever heard. One time he was talking about a young girl who killed herself over a young man. The pastor called the young lady stupid, and he went on and on about her. I felt bad and felt everyone was thinking about my son who had just died at the time it was said. After service I spoke to him and told him how I felt, and he apologized to me. I know the pastor is not trying to hurt me, but I don't understand his thinking. Today, I am depressed. I have sought counselling, but I didn't feel it helped me. The counsellor did not know much about suicide. I do feel guilty at times, because the night before my son died he told me he was in pain. I know he was feeling a little down, but never did I believe he would take his own life. I have a website at: kevinscause.org. I hope to help others in any way that I can.

A little over a year before my son died he was jumped on when he was leaving for work. It was a lot of guys who beat him in the head, stabbed him with a pencil and fractured his spine. My son spent a week in the ICU because he was bleeding in the head. After that incident my son had changed. He could not find a job once he started feeling better. Kevin started getting headaches, and he started using drugs. He was involved in a relationship with a girl who was abusive mentally and physically. She would scratch his face up whenever she'd get mad. However, he'd gotten arrested for eight months, and after he got out of jail he was no longer using drugs. He saw how crazy this girl was and wanted to get away from her. Kevin complained of headaches, but he seemed to be doing okay.

Approximately two months before he died he started saying he was a little depressed. I thought it had a lot to do with wanting to get away from this girl and she was like a fatal attraction. It's a long story, however Kevin was going to group counselling and that was through the court. I told his probation officer that Kevin seems a little depressed, and she told my son he needed to snap out of it. Well a month later he took his life.

I had my husband talk with him the night

before he died because he told me he was in pain. My husband talked with him and told him not to worry about a job and that he could stay with us as long as he wanted. The morning he died his girlfriend had called and I heard him go into the garage and he never came out. The night before he died, he asked me to take him to his counselling because his car was broke, and I was going to take him.

I don't understand what went wrong. I don't understand the brain and why, why, why this happened! Your article I read today helped me a lot. I am going to buy your book too. Again, thank you. Wanda Jackson, Kevin's mom.
(This an example of a suicide situation one of my readers shared with me)

Kevin was not the only victim in the above illustration. Society, and in particular the church, has an opportunity to be loving and sensitive to families of suicide victims. As well we need to expand our understanding of what we can do to assist victims of suicide and the wounded communities left in their wake.

In the following "A Theology of Suicide" we will find some consolation for the families and friends of suicide victims.

A Theology of Suicide

At the end of this chapter I will share information

about suicide that can be found in pamphlets or on-line. What you may not find there are the spiritual and moral implications of such a desperate and unnatural act. The Christian church traditionally has not always handled this question well. Fortunately more recent theology has been more compassionate and Christ-like.

As a child, my first experiences with suicide left me with a terrible sense of desolation. When a neighbour of mine committed suicide, I was devastated. I had heard too much about judgement and damnation and not enough about love and redemption. I did not know that most suicides are a result of illness, mental or otherwise. I did not know that suicide takes the victim out of life against his or her will. I did not know that God's mercy is still available to these most unfortunate victims.

A mother of a suicide victim once said that if she could only bring back her child for a moment, she would put her arms around her and hug her and never let her go. This mother is showing love, not judgement. And the great news is that God's love is greater than that of a mother. God's arms are always open to the lost and the victim. Christ came to die for the sinner, not the just.

Doors cannot shut out the love of Christ. The Resurrected Christ appeared to the frightened disciples in the upper room. He passed through the doors they had bolted in fear and greeted them with, "Peace be with you." The same Christ descended into the realm of the dead to open the gates of hell to free us from the hold of death.

The suicide victim who only sees the darkness of life is still most certainly loved by Christ. It is for victims like this that Christ died and descended into hell. How can we doubt the power of his love to rescue a loved one from the desolation of such a death? Christ's arms remain open and his love is boundless. His greeting is, "Peace be with you!"

Christ has the power to pass through doors that a suicide victim may inadvertently close. Christ came to die for thieves, for sinners, for us and for suicide victims. I cannot imagine his love would cease for one who is most destitute, helpless and lost. I can imagine his open arms!

I will give the final word in this chapter to Father Ron Rolheiser who has influenced my theology on suicide. When all is read and done, suicide is still so devastating that we must reach to God for help. The process of mourning is much more difficult and painful. All the consolation we can gather from the Church, from Scripture and from our relationship with God is needed. Family and community support and understanding is paramount.

In "Struggling to Understand Suicide" Father Ron summarizes some of the points we covered earlier:

> "So what's to be said about suicide? … Understanding suicide more compassionately won't take away its sting … but our own long-term healing and the redemption of the memory of the one who died can be helped by keeping a number of things in mind.
>
> Suicide, in most cases, is a disease, not something freely-willed. The person who dies in this way dies against his or her will, akin to those who jumped to their deaths from the Twin Towers after terrorist planes had set those buildings on fire …. They were jumping to certain death, but only because they were already burning to death where

they were standing.

Death by suicide is analogous to death by cancer, stroke, or heart-attack; except, in the case of suicide, it's a question of emotional-cancer, emotional-stroke, or an emotional heart attack.

Moreover, still to be more fully explored, is the potential role that biochemistry plays in suicide. Since some suicidal depressions are treatable by drugs, clearly then some suicides are caused by biochemical deficiencies, as are many other diseases that kill us.

The person who dies in this way, almost invariably, is a very sensitive human being. Suicide is rarely done in arrogance, as an act of contempt .... Generally our own experience with the loved ones that we've lost to suicide is that these persons were anything but arrogant. More accurately described, they were too bruised to touch and were wounded in some deep way that we couldn't comprehend or help heal ....

Finally, we need not worry unduly about the eternal salvation of those who die in this way. God's understanding and compassion infinitely surpasses our own. Our lost loved ones are in safer hands than ours. If we, limited as we are, can already reach through this tragedy with some understanding and love, we can rest secure in the fact that, given the width and depth of God's love, the one who dies through suicide meets, on the other side, a compassion that's deeper than our own and a judgment that intuits the deepest motives of their heart.

Father Ron goes on to describe the suicide victim as someone who is "standing inside an oak-like door, shut in because of fear, wound, sickness, or loneliness. Most persons who die by suicide are precisely locked inside this kind of private room by some cancerous wound through which we cannot reach and through which they themselves cannot reach.

"We cannot reach them. But we know through Christ's Resurrection that he passes through closed doors to … stand inside the huddle of fear and loneliness and breathe out peace." (Luke 24:36).

Suicide: Prevention and Statistics

As a sort of appendix I offer the following brief notes I have compiled from a community workshop on suicide and other research over the years. Prevention of suicide is a primary goal. If you feel suicidal, talk to family and friends, talk to a help center, and talk to a doctor (clinical depression can be treated). Statistics Canada shares the following information on the causes of suicide:

> Research shows that mental illness is the most important risk factor for suicide; and that more than 90% of people who commit suicide have a mental or addictive disorder. Depression is the most common illness among those who die from suicide,

with approximately 60% suffering from this condition. No single determinant, including mental illness, is enough on its own to cause a suicide. Rather, suicide typically results from the interaction of many factors, for example: mental illness, marital breakdown, financial hardship, deteriorating physical health, a major loss, or a lack of social support.

At the practical level the opportunity to help others is significant. The most important thing you must do is listen. You cannot take away their grief and sadness, but you can support them. Talk to them. Talk to their family and friends. Talk to a help center or a doctor. Clinical depression can be treated.

A Health District Checklist of first-aid hints for suicide prevention includes the following:

Be Observant – know and recognize warning signs. Pay attention to your suspicions. Trust your judgement.

Check It Out – Inquire about less noticeable signs. Ask others about what they have noticed.

Reach Out to the Person – Show you care. Hear what they are saying. Tell them what you have noticed.

Ask About Suicide – Ask directly about suicidal intentions.

Show Respect – Be as understanding as possible. Be honest and genuine. Take the situation seriously.

Be Actively Involved – Talk openly and freely. Ask direct questions.

Determine Risk – Ask about previous attempts and ideations (thoughts about suicide). Ask for the details of the suicide plan.

Offer Support – Let them talk. Focus specifically on doing something about suicide. Offer realistic hope. Identify other supports such as parents, friends, counsellors, family and crisis lines.

Get Help – Urge the person to get help. Be firm about your intentions to get help for them if they won't. Avoid secrecy pacts. Don't leave if the risk of suicide is high.

Warning signs may include a previous attempt, a threat of suicide, depression, talk of death ("I can't go on"), tension, social withdrawal, drug or alcohol abuse, sleep irregularities, feeling worthless, recent loss or life change, reckless behaviour, getting affairs in order, or giving away valued possessions.

Causes of suicide may be one or more of the following:

Genetic factors - manic depression in one parent may lead to a 27% chance of a child getting it.

Psycho-social Factor – death of a loved one; stressful experience; learned negative experiences such as pessimism, hopelessness, negative self evaluation.

Biological Factors –no consistent finding, but may include hormonal abnormalities; testosterone levels in males may be depressed; neurotransmitters (chemical messengers to the brain) such as lack of serotonin can lead to depression.

Psychotherapy as well as chemical therapy may be required to effect a continued cure. A second or subsequent episodes of depression may indicate several months of medication.

Know the facts: suicide is among the three leading

causes of death among those age 15-45 (both sexes); 90% of all suicide cases are associated with mental disorder; more die from suicide than homicide; suicide rates worldwide have risen 60 % in the past 45 years. Source: **World Health Organization.**

Other facts to remember: 1) spring and fall are peak seasons for suicides; 2) males are three times as successful at suicide attempts; 3) the cause of suicide is unknown, though genetic factors, psychosocial factors and biological factors may all play a role.

Suicide prevention is related to cause. Sometimes the temporary problem has a solution. It may be biochemical – depression can be treated with drugs. Most often professional help is required, and timely intervention steps need to be taken. Know the numbers to call and procedures to follow. If there is immediate danger, call 911 or other assistance. Family is often the first level of intervention, but it is also where guilt most often remains. Fact: the suicide victim picks a time and place that makes final intervention impossible.

Chapter 11

Palliative Care, Euthanasia and a Happy Death

How do we see the Good News of Jesus in the

suffering of Covid-19 patients, palliative care, euthanasia and dying? Once we understand the meaning of suffering and the cross, and God's gift of death as a "healing medicine", as St Ambrose put it, then we can look forward to a good death.

There is an ancient legend which holds that when an infant is created God kisses its soul and sings to it. As its guardian angel carries it to earth to join its body, she also sings to it. The legend says that God's kiss and his song, as well as the song of the angel, remain in that soul forever – to be called up, cherished, shared, and to become the basis of all our songs.

In the very first episode of *Breaking Bad*, Walter White tells his students that the essence of chemistry and life itself is "growth, then decay, then transformation." In her column "Walter White's Life lessons — Breaking Bad" Natarro (Nikki Tarrant-Hoskins) says if you believe in the transformation of life, getting through the days of nursing someone with a terminal illness will no doubt be easier. You can cling to the faith that as a primary care giver, you're helping your loved one past the pain and suffering of their final journey. That is a privilege and a responsibility.

In a related article Tarrant-Hoskins says,

> "What could you say to a dying person that would not enrage by its triviality? It all has the most profound purpose and meaning. Will there ever be a more important time or place?
>
> "The last breath, the last heartbeat, the wrenching open of the veil that moves our loved one away from pain forever. Words do

not matter. Being there matters. There is no right or wrong, so you don't have to worry about getting it right.

"You just have to show up. There will never be another moment that compares to this in life … the last kiss, the last embrace, the last conscious moment that you'll ever share. Don't squander a word, a syllable; don't squander a second."

To be a witness to the transformation of life, the reunion of a soul with its maker, is a moment to be cherished, remembered and shared. As Christians who hope in God's promises, we give thanks at a journey completed, a destiny attained. Though the world may seem empty, we "Let God's promises shine on your problems." Corrie Ten Boom.

"Darkness cannot put out the Light. It can only make God brighter." -Author Unknown

Palliative Care – Father Mark Miller Workshop

What would you not do to alleviate the struggle and pain of a spouse, parent, child? That is what this chapter is about – what we can do. Maybe we haven't thought about it before. There is good news. No, there is no reprieve; we will all die eventually. But with palliative care we do not have to die alone or in unbearable pain. Good planning can make the process of dying more natural.

I am going to share notes from a workshop on *Proper Care of the Dying* presented in Preeceville, August 31, 2016, by Redemptorist Father Mark Miller. Miller spent some sixteen years at St. Paul's Hospital in Saskatoon caring for the dying. Miller shared that "dying is natural". Things happen in the lives of the dying that are extremely important to the family and the dying member. That is why assisted suicide is not good and is not natural.

In a brief history on dying Miller said that in the 1950's 70% of the people died at home. By the 1970's people were dying in hospitals, and since the 1990's many die in palliative care. It is important that patients be allowed to "live" while they are dying. Hospice care can provide a non-hospital place for the dying.

Today there is still much to learn about dying and the process of living while you are dying. There is music and art therapy. Some learn to paint, to fulfill dreams and do creative things in that end stage of life.

Fear of pain is perhaps the greatest fear of the dying. In Canada today, Miller said, there is no need to die of unbearable pain. Morphine and other drugs will provide relief. Struggling for breath is a second anxiety. The use of respirators can help to alleviate that situation.

Father Miller shared the example of a dying mother who was breathing at 5%. Everyone was tense and worried about her shortness of breath. The doctor administered a sedative that night; she relaxed and had a restful night. When the family came in the morning she sat up, looked each one in the eye, smiled, and then passed away peacefully.

There is so much to learn about dying, and the dying members teach the family about this natural process.

Things happen in the lives of the dying that are extremely important to the family and to the person dying. Father Mark shared the example of a mother of six whose children had become estranged. They would not speak to each other, and no one would visit the mother if another sibling was there. When the mother was unconscious the nurse contacted the children individually, since they did not have each other's phone numbers. First one of them came and held the mother's hand. Then a daughter came and held the other hand. A son arrived. Eventually all six were there. Then the mother died. Her work was finished. She had brought her children together in a final act of grace.

Another example Miller shared involved a forty-two-year-old businessman who had just been diagnosed with terminal cancer. "I have the right to be bitter," he said angrily. His had a twenty-five-million-dollar business, and he was just ready to work less and get to know his family. In the two and a half weeks he had left he got to know them and love them. He told his nurse, "This cancer was a gift."

In another example shared by Miller, a mother had to depend on her children for care. "I just hate being dependant," she said. Her son pointed out how she helped them when they were babies. Now it was their turn to help her.

Palliative care support is so important to patients to let them know they are human. Only thirty per cent of Canadian patients get palliative care. "We are here to care for people, not kill them," Miller said. The need for expanded palliative care is a serious issue right now. Under-funding palliative care is not acceptable, Miller insists.

We need to reassure patients we will look after them. There are benefits to dying in a natural way. Miller shared the example of a dying man who just wanted to "get it over with". The Nurse asked him, "Do your grand children know who you are?" The man spent his last three weeks writing an autobiography to let his family know who he was.

Advance planning is beneficial to all. A good death involves setting up health care directives in the event they are needed. This leads us into considering the ethics of our treatment plans. Miller set out some basic principles to help us determine moral choices. A first principle, he said, is that it is OK to die; but it is not OK to kill someone. You do not have to use a ventilator to prolong the dying. You can refuse treatment at any time and follow nature's way. If morphine gets people out of pain, you may use it; even if it risks shortening life.

We have two great fears about dying, Miller said. The first is pain and suffering, and the second is fear of abandonment. Palliative care addresses both these fears.

Pain relief is OK, Miller said. Pain and suffering can be helped by palliative care. That is a moral choice. We do not need to be trapped in the system that is trying to save us. Sometimes doctors have difficulty letting go and allowing a patient to die. There are feeding tubes, ventilators, and always one more drug to try. The record for feeding tube was set by a patient who used it for thirty-nine years. You can refuse any procedure or treatment. Some religious groups refuse blood transfusions. A cancer patient may refuse surgery, radiation or chemo. You have the final say on accepting treatment, Miller insisted.

"People have a right to refuse medical

treatment. The right to refuse medical treatment is not the same as an act of assisted suicide and does not constitute euthanasia. When medical treatment is withheld or withdrawn, sometimes the person dies quickly, sometimes the person dies after a few days or weeks, and sometimes the person does not die at all. If the person dies, they die from their medical condition ....

"Sometimes people experience intractable [uncontrollable] pain which can be effectively relieved through sedation. The proper use of sedation is intended to eliminate the pain and not kill the person, whereas, euthanasia or assisted suicide intends to kill the person."
(from *Protecting People From Euthanasia & Assisted Suicide* ALLIANCE for LIFE – SASKATOON, INC.)

Have a "living will" in place in case it is needed. Do you want to refuse resuscitation at some point? Do you want to refuse antibiotics at some point? You may cure the pneumonia only to have the cancer kill you. You can say yes or no to any treatment.

You should have a family member appointed to make your wishes known if you get to the point of not being able to express them. If you do not appoint someone, your spouse or the oldest child will be your guardian. Perhaps you would like a younger child to have that responsibility? You can choose. Know that you have autonomy – you get to decide treatment options. But you do not get to choose to end your life unethically. There are moral principles at play.

Again, you do not have to choose to prolong the dying process. You can refuse feeding tubes and ventilators. You can refuse resuscitation at some point in your health care. And you can appoint a family member to see that your wishes are known when you are in an unconscious state.

In conclusion, there is good news about dying. It is a natural process and can be a positive and learning experience for family members. The two greatest fears about dying, pain / suffering and fear of abandonment, can be looked after with appropriate care giving or palliative care.

Euthanasia and a Happy Death

A youth asked his 96-year-old dad, "What is the secret of your longevity?" The dad answered, "It's simple, son. I take one quarter teaspoon of gunpowder every day." The lad thought he would try it, and sure enough he too lived to be 96 years old. And when he died he left behind him eight children, 32 grandchildren, 86 great grand children and a sixteen-foot hole in the wall of the crematorium.

Perhaps the reader will be more comfortable with the description "a good death" rather than a happy death, but in my family circle when we prayed the family rosary every night we often prayed for a "happy death". I do believe my parents both had a happy death with glorious results. Faith can give you that.

A good death, Miller said, is that you are looked after properly; pain is controlled; family relationships are supportive, and you know that you are loved. As with all things in life, preparation is the key to smooth transitions.

Have you ever thought of the Gift of Death? That death is a blessing? In Geoffrey Chaucer's "The Pardoner's Tale" we see an old man seeking his grave, knocking on the ground saying, "O my dear mother [earth], let me in! When shall my bones come to their rest?"

St Ambrose said, "God did not will death in the beginning; he gave it rather as a healing medicine. For once man was condemned to lasting toil for his sins, his life became wretched; there had to be an end to the misery so that death might restore man's original condition [immortal life]."

Euthanasia and the Good News

"What a lovely funeral!" my aunt used to say on the occasion of a faith-filled death and burial. As children we puzzled over that. In time and by natural process we absorbed the philosophy of our parents and elders so we too understood a meaningful and blessed end to life.

There is much purpose and healing in suffering. Christ on the cross was not looking for euthanasia. Christians in particular understand the meaning of suffering.

Thank you, Jesus! Thank you for inviting us to help sinners with our suffering. As Christians we are asked to "take up the cross" of daily suffering, of pain, of illness. We unite our suffering to the Cross of Christ for our salvation and that of the world.

A friend in Australia shared these thoughts on her brother's dying. "My brother is … sleeping mostly, but in his moments of clarity, is intensely captivating. As painful as it is to watch him fade, there is so much healing taking place in his suffering, and ours. If one could bottle it, we would have the answer to all the unrest and chaos, loneliness and neglect that the world must hold. While some would be thinking of euthanasia, we are thinking only of love. The power in that humble bush home is tangible. Real love at work in its purest form."

Christ's dying sacrifice was real love at work in its purest form. That LOVE is, in fact, the answer to all the unrest and chaos, loneliness and neglect that the world can hold. As Christians we are invited to unite our pain and suffering, and ultimately our dying, to that sacrifice of the Cross.

But all is not cross and dross in the life of the Christian. *Dross* is used here in the sense of wicked people whom God removes in judgment, and impurities in believers which are removed by discipline and trials. No, the creator gives us much more joy in life; a joie de vivre embracing all the beauty and pleasure of creation. After a full life and the normal processes of aging we eventually turn towards that natural end of our earthly existence.

Father Miller was very clear about his condemnation of assisted suicide to end life. Dying is a natural event. Killing someone is not. So much happens in the final hours for the dying and for their families. Doctor assisted suicide is unnatural and can become the standard, Miller warned. Elderly people may feel that they are a burden and an expense to their families. There is a real danger here, especially when you consider diminished mental capacity in medical conditions the elderly face. Alzheimer's comes to mind. Who safeguards the natural dying process where the law allows assisted suicide?

We get so much from the dying we care for. "We need the dying to be our teachers," Miller said. There are moral and ethical considerations surrounding the end of life. Assisted suicide falls short of the ideal of a good death or a happy death.

Euthanasia and assisted suicide are unsafe. Government statistics say that 70% of elder abusers are people on whom the abused depend. In Belgium where euthanasia is legal a study in May found that 32% of the euthanasia deaths in Flanders were done without request or consent. Another study in Belgium October 2010 said 47% of euthanasia deaths were not reported. Under reporting was often linked to questionable deaths.

> "Is it possible to protect people who are depressed? A pro-euthanasia oncologist in the Netherlands, where euthanasia is legal, published a study on depression and euthanasia in September 2005. She found that people who were depressed or had 'feelings of extreme hopelessness' were 4.1 times more likely to request euthanasia. The report concluded that *depression is a primary factor for requests for euthanasia.*"
> (from *Protecting People From Euthanasia &*

"Sometimes people believe in little or nothing, and yet they give their lives to that little or nothing. One life is all we have, and we live it as we believe in living it and then it's gone. But to surrender what we are and to live without belief is more terrible than dying – even dying young." St Joan of Arc.

Chapter 12
Joy and Hope

"How beautiful on the mountains, are the feet of one who brings good news" (Isaiah 52:7).

A boy sat on a park bench loudly exclaiming, "Hallelujah! Hallelujah! God is great!" A university graduate asked the boy about his joy. "I just read that God led the whole nation of Israel right through the middle of the Red Sea."

The man laughed and said, "Science has shown that the Red Sea was only 10-inches deep at that time." The boy thought for a while and exclaimed, "Wow! God is greater than I thought! Not only did He lead Israel through the Red Sea, but He drowned the whole Egyptian army in 10 inches of water!"

What keeps us from the simple joy of the evangelical boy in this story? Why do we so often wish we were someone else? Anyone else? Others look like their lives are so much better, so much more successful. Father Brendan McGuire said: There is nothing more unbelievable than a "joyless Christian." When you think about it, if you really believe in the cross, if you really believe that Christ Jesus has come to save us, and the message is here and now, then surely our lives have to be transformed by joy. Because we know that salvation is ours, our actions then must demonstrate to the world that our lives are different because of that knowledge. If we do not have that joy, then how can people really believe us?

In this desperate Covid-19 time we must let the joy of the Resurrection lift us up! Isaiah 26:12-19 says: "My soul yearns for you in the night … O Lord, you will ordain peace for us … Your dead shall live; their corpses will rise. O Dwellers in the dust, awake and sing for joy!"

Joy to the World

When did I become a Christian? Didn't *Christian* begin with *Christmas*? My Christmas experiences as a child were events of joy. I still renew that joy every Christmas as I celebrate the beginning of my Christian life.

One of my fondest Christmas Eve memories is 1955 when we left Midnight Mass and literally went "dashing through the snow" by bobsled, in a blizzard, to get back to the farm two miles away. The neighbors raced alongside

129

with their Standard Bred team trying to pass us for the first quarter mile or so, until the trails blended into one. The roads were blocked until March with six-foot drifts of snow.

In my childhood heart I felt the true joy of Christmas. Christmas was <u>home</u>, a place to warm frostbitten toes and fingers, to relish sweet food, to enjoy gifts purchased in the most frugal fashion (socks, shirts); a place where there was security and peace that sprang from a spiritual wholeness of good living in a great family.

Today Covid-19 forms a depression in our world, a surround, to use a poetic word. Millions have died and the scourge goes on. Yet the hope of the Christian is greater than all this.

"God and his son, Jesus, await me in a better place, so I can look forward to the time when I go home, when I will be free again, free in a way as never before," writes death-row inmate David Paul Hammer of Oklahoma. "God forgave me the second I asked him to," David says. "God has removed hate, anger and bitterness... [and] replaced these feelings with love, peace and commitment."

The Joy of Christians is with us since we opened the gift of Christmas! That gift, the Incarnation and Redemption, conquers death and can touch the inner restlessness and longing of our hearts. There is nothing that we cannot put into Christ's hands so that our burden will be lighter. We have carried some of these burdens by ourselves too long. The Covid night which surrounds us can become a "silent night", where "all is holy", and by some Christmas miracle "all is bright".

We need to focus on the brighter side. "Yesterday is history. Tomorrow is mystery. Today is a gift. That's why it is called the <u>present</u>." I'm not sure of the source of this quote, but I heard it recently at the funeral of a close friend who celebrated life even as he was dying of cancer.

We need to travel light on our journey to the Father. When Jesus sent out the seventy disciples to every town and place to proclaim the Good News he said, "Carry no purse, no bag, no sandals; and greet no one on the road." (Luke 10:1-12). So little is essential to sustain us. But if you have helped anyone move lately, you know how many truckloads of baggage we normally carry with us.

We not only need to travel physically lighter, but we need to have a light heart as we travel on our pilgrimage. Jesus said to the seventy disciples and he says to us: "I watched Satan fall from heaven like a flash of lightning. See, I have given you authority to tread on snakes and scorpions… Nothing will hurt you …rejoice that your names are written in heaven." (Luke 10:18-20).

We have great cause for rejoicing! We should be trembling at the tremendous power and authority Jesus gives us as he invites us to further the Kingdom. Satan has been brought low and our freedom has been bought. Rejoice and believe the Good News.

The world is crying out to hear Good News! Our everyday world feeds us enough disappointment, deception and despair to disillusion most. Check the political campaigns during election time. Is there hope and good news? How easily we can get mired into the mud.

My concern is that if we are not careful, we can become an obstacle to the message of joy and hope that Christ wants us to impart to others. That would be a pity. It is such a pleasant task to bring good news!

Living in God's Peace

Do you want to be happy? Filled with joy? It is no secret that the joy of Christ's message is thriving best in Third World countries, among the poorest of the poor. To them God's words in Isaiah 55 are easier to understand, though they bring much consolation to everyone of faith:

"Oh, come to the water all you who are thirsty;
though you have no money, come!
Buy corn without money, and eat,
And, at no cost, wine and milk.
Why spend your money on what is not bread,
Your wages on what fails to satisfy?
Listen, listen to me, and you will have good things to eat
And rich food to enjoy.
Pay attention, come to me;
Listen, and your soul will live."

True peace will come to those who, like St. Francis of Assisi, become a channel of Christ's peace. Where there is hatred, they sow love; where there is injury, they bring forgiveness; where there is doubt and fear, they bring faith; where there is sadness, they bring joy; where there is despair, they bring hope; and where there is darkness, they bring light.

The story is told of St. Francis of Assisi who one day met an acquaintance who looked troubled and asked him: "Brother, how are things with you?" The man started raving, "Thanks to my master – May God curse him! – I have had nothing but misfortune. He has taken away all I possess."

Francis, filled with pity, said, "Brother, pardon your master for the love of God, and free your own soul; it's possible that he will restore to you whatever he has taken away. Otherwise, you have lost your goods and will lose your soul as well." But the man persisted, "I can't fully forgive him unless he returns what he has taken from me." Francis insisted, "Look, I will give you this cloak; I beg you to forgive your master for the love of the Lord God." The man's heart melted by this kindness and he forgave his master. Immediately he was filled with joy.

Like St Francis, our role is to serve others as Christ would. By spreading the joy and freedom that we are heirs to as followers of Christ, we become the arms of Christ reaching out to a world which desperately needs peace and joy. The warmth of that embrace can bring joy and peace, no matter how desperate the situation of our lives.

Living in Hope

"The word that God has written in the brow of every person is hope." -Victor Hugo.

At Bethlehem the Angels proclaimed *Joy* and *Peace* to a world living in the hope of a Saviour. Our job as Christians is to live that Joy and Peace and to share that hope with the world.

Joy and Peace begin with Hope. Hope is to trust, to wait for, to want something good or beneficial in the future, like heaven. Hope is also to have reason to believe it might be so. The Kingdom of God will come. Our world

133

will be changed.

For centuries before the coming of Christ, prophets proclaimed the hope of the Saviour's coming. That hope was fulfilled by the Angels' proclamation on Christmas night: "Glory to God in the highest heaven, and on earth peace to those on whom his favor rests". With that song, which came literally from Angels in heaven, the earth was filled with *joy*. The Kingdom of God had come. Our world is still changing. As Christians we need to wear shades; the future is so bright! Our joy is happiness over a present good which is perhaps beyond what we anticipated. This spiritual happiness is over our salvation and the bliss of the afterlife.

The tragedy of our world is that many struggle just to get by each day when they could be alive in hope. We need to rest in Jesus. When we work with Jesus as his disciples, we enter into his rest, and that is a rest free from worries and troubles. Let God DO and let God BE. "Be still and know that I am God." (Psalm 46:10).

> "God is still writing your story. Quit trying to steal the pen. Trust the author."
> (topradio.ro)

The peace in the work of our daily lives comes from leaving in God's hands what we can't do with our hands. We are co-partners with God in our work, our families and our lives. We who *believe* enter that rest! (Hebrews 4:3). The Holy Spirit gives us strength to do all things through Christ.

"Come to me, all you who are weary and burdened,

And I will give you rest. Take my yoke upon you and learn

From me, for I am gentle and humble of heart, and you will

Find rest for your souls. For my yoke is easy and my burden

Is light." (Matthew 11:28-33).

Living a life in peace and rest with the Lord is best described in Psalm 23:

> The Lord is my shepherd, I lack nothing.
> He makes me lie down in green pastures,
> he leads me beside quiet waters,
> he refreshes my soul.
> He guides me along the right paths
> for his name's sake.
> Even though I walk
> through the darkest valley,
> I will fear no evil,
> for you are with me;
> your rod and your staff,
> they comfort me.
> You prepare a table before me
> in the presence of my enemies.
> You anoint my head with oil;
> my cup overflows.
> Surely your goodness and love will follow me
> all the days of my life,
> and I will dwell in the house of the Lord

forever.

Cling to God's peace and seek God's goodness and love. Laughter and tears are our lot in life; as frequent as the sunshine and the rain. My Russian German parents had a saying that sometimes we have laughter and tears in the same bag. Kahlil Gibran put it this way:

> "Some of you say, 'Joy is greater than sorrow,' and others say, 'Nay, sorrow is the greater'. But I say unto you, they are inseparable. Together they come, and when one sits alone with you at your board, remember that the other is asleep upon your bed."

Chapter 13
Pain and Suffering

It may seem to us that we are living our lives surrounded by a Covid-19 landscape. The fact is we are still in view of the infinite horizon, the boundless promise of God.

There's a Buddhist parable that runs something like this:

> *One day as the Buddha was sitting under a tree, a young, trim soldier walked by, looked at the Buddha, noticed his weight and his fat, and said: "You look like a pig!" The Buddha looked up calmly at the soldier and said: "And you look like God!"*

Taken aback by the comment, the soldier asked the Buddha: "Why do you say that I look like God?" The Buddha replied: "Well, we don't really see what's outside of ourselves, we see what's inside of us and project it out. I sit under this tree all day and I think about God, so that when I look out, that's what I see. And you, you must be thinking about other things!"

How we see the world on a given day is deeply influenced and coloured by our own interiority. Perhaps that should give us insight into those days when we feel sad, depressed or anything but grateful for God's tremendous gift of life. We cannot be unhappy if we are filled with gratitude, but we can be happy even when we are in pain. Pain is a part of living. Facing the challenges of pain helps us to continue maturing.

Pain and Suffering

Father Murphy walks into a pub in Donegal and asks the first man he meets, "Do you want to go to heaven?"
The man said, "I do, Father."
The priest said, "Then stand over there against the wall."
Then the priest asked the second man, "Do you want to go to heaven?"
"Certainly, Father," the man replied.
"Then stand over there against the wall," said the priest.

*Then Father Murphy walked up to
O'Toole and asked, "Do you want to go to
heaven?"*

O'Toole said, "No, I don't Father."

*The priest said, "I don't believe this.
You mean to tell me that when you die you
don't want to go to heaven?"*

*O'Toole said, "Oh, when I die, yes. I
thought you were getting a group together to
go right now."*

Most of us are like O'Toole when the Lord asks us to bear suffering and pain. We know we will die some day, but meanwhile we like to say no to the invitation to pain. We want to accept the Cross, but not right now! And that is normal. But it is most important to have an understanding about suffering when it does visit us or those we love.

You may have heard of the story of the actor who rehearsed his one line, "Hark, I hear a cannon shot". He was to say this after the cannon was fired. For days he repeated the line, "Hark, I hear a cannon shot". The night of the actual performance when the cannon was fired, he said, "What the hell was that?"

The Cross

You and I reflect on the agony of Christ on the Cross. We study and ponder its meaning and the meaning of suffering in our lives. But when real suffering comes along, when we meet the Cross in our lives and face real pain, we say, "What the hell was that?"

138

When I was a child I used to say a prayer after Communion that included: "From this moment I accept whatsoever death Thou shalt send me, with its sorrows and afflictions [and a few other words I did not understand at the time] and in union with Christ I offer this up in reparation for my sins and the sins of the whole world."

What I am about to say may sound foolish in terms of the values of this world, but we should rejoice when we see that first sign of arthritis that comes with age. We should rejoice at that first bout with cancer. Recently, after jogging, I could feel a pain in my ankles and realized I was no longer a spry seventy-year-old. But to me the tingle in my ankles and the stiff muscles when I get up in the morning are a sign of the victory to come. I realize it is very easy to be cerebral in the absence of real pain, but it is still a matter of perspective.

As I write this, I am grateful for all that I have realized in the years since my prostate cancer surgery. Having emerged from a "cancer" sentence has enriched my life as I appreciate more fully the tremendous blessings of family, friends, grandchildren and the innumerable gifts that start with the sunrise every morning.

Eventually death will take us. I am reminded of my late brother's comment to his doctor: "You're not a very good doctor. All your patients are going to die." We will lose the battle for good health and fitness. Cancer or Alzheimer's is not the end, but the beginning.

Death is not the end but the beginning. Our moment of death will be the greatest moment of our existence. It will be the time to rejoice in Christ's victory over death. Our deliverance from despair is found in the Cross. Paradoxically the Cross may look like Love dying, but it is turning despair into hope. Look at that Cross in your suffering and pain, in that time before death that we will all have to face.

The greatest meditation related to pain and suffering is to reflect on the Passion of Jesus. Our Lord said to St Bernard, "I will remit all the venial sins and I will no more think of the mortal sins of those who honour the grievous wound on my right shoulder, which caused me unutterable pain when bearing my heavy cross to Calvary." (*Passion of Christ Material* from Ave Maria Centre of Peace, Toronto).

And it works. For some time now I have had arthritic pain in my neck It is harder to make shoulder checks when driving, but with continued exercise and some dietary supplements I am enjoying some relief. But whenever the neck pain bothers me, or an old shoulder pain comes back, I think of the cross and Jesus' sore shoulder. That brings me great comfort as I think of Jesus' words to St Bernard.

Our Lord revealed to several holy women, St Gertrude, St Bridget, St Mechtilde and to St Catharine of Siena, that they who meditate on his Passion are very dear to him. St Augustine writes that "there is no more profitable occupation for the soul than to meditate daily on the Passion of Our Lord." St Bonaventure says that "he who desires to go on advancing from virtue to virtue, from grace to grace, should meditate continually on the Passion of Jesus."

The Saints say that five minutes of prayer in honour of the Passion is of greater value than many hours spent in other devotions. St Alphonse says that all the Saints became saints by devotion to the Passion, and that there was no saint who did not have a great love of the Passion. The key to finding meaning in suffering is being close to God.

Mystery of suffering

Where is God when there is suffering and pain? Why do bad things happen to good people? A reporter once asked Mother Teresa of Calcutta, "Where is God when a baby child dies alone in a back alley?" And Mother Teresa tersely answered the question, "God is right there with the child in that dark alley. The more important question is, 'Where are you?'"

A deeper meaning to suffering is hinted at in Mark 8 when Jesus tells the disciples that he must undergo great suffering and be put to death. Peter argues with Jesus about this. Jesus says, "Get behind me, Satan! For you are setting your mind not on divine things but on human things." Christ's suffering was for the salvation of all. Our suffering can be part of this salvation plan as we offer it for our sins and the redemption of all.

At its deepest level, suffering is a mystery. Where there is suffering, Christ is close by. When the thief hung on the cross, Jesus said, "This day you will be with me in Paradise". Here we enjoy the emotional distance to recognize the Cross of Calvary as it applies to human suffering. It is a little harder to accept when a loved one is suffering.

Pain and suffering are foolishness to the world. To the Christian they are a profound mystery. The Christian finds the redemptive and intercessory power of suffering. Christ showed us the way. Job said, "For I know that my vindicator lives … and from my flesh I shall see God." (Job 19:25, 26).

That which is darkness and death is also light and

life! Pain and tears give way to a banquet of joy, where every tear will be wiped away. This could be a metaphor for our earth before the birth of Christ. Our world of struggle, pain, sin and much needed redemption received the gift of the Incarnation. Christ came to redeem our nature and our world.

Knowing that "God is with us" helps us celebrate despite the pain. Our darkness of illness, death, pain, loneliness and all that flesh is heir to gives way to hope and joy. "If it [the joy] be not now, yet it will come", as Hamlet said. "The readiness is all".

> The incarnation does not promise heaven on earth. It promises heaven in heaven. Here, on earth, it promises us something else – God's presence in our lives. This presence redeems because knowing that God is with us is what ultimately empowers us to give up bitterness, to forgive, and to move beyond cynicism and bitterness. When God is with us then pain and happiness are not mutually exclusive, and the agonies and riddles of life do not exclude deep meaning and deep joy. (from "Incarnation – God is With Us" 2016 Christmas article by Father Ron Rolheiser.)

The story is told of the French impressionist Auguste Renoir's last years of paralyzing arthritis. Henri Matisse visited him daily, watching Renoir fighting torturous pain with each brush stroke. Finally Matisse asked, "Auguste, why do you continue to paint when you are in such agony?"

"The pain passes but the beauty remains," Renoir replied. Indeed, the pain of the Cross passes but the beauty of the Resurrection light remains. Without Christ's light we stumble in darkness.

We need to focus on the beauty of the Resurrection and the joy of the new life Jesus created for us, and not the pain of the crucifixion? Why do we not look beyond the Cross at the life Jesus promised Dismas: "Today you will be with me in Paradise"?

> "I am the Resurrection. If anyone believes in
> me, even though he dies he will live. And
> whoever believes in me will never die."
> (John 11:25-26).

Our Suffering and Purgatory

The pain passes, but the beauty remains. Our suffering and, ultimately, dying will provide a purgatory for us and for those for whom we offer our atonement. Purgatory is an often misunderstood concept and can be troubling even to people of faith. St Catherine of Genoa explains it this way, "As for paradise, God has placed no doors there. Whoever wishes to enter, does so. An all-merciful God stands there with His arms open, waiting to receive us into His Glory."

Saint Catherine goes on to explain that the divine presence is so pure that any soul with still the least imperfection will seek purification before entering into God's presence. In our lives we live with the knowledge

143

of redemption by the on-going work of Christ, ever combating the effects of original sin in our world. And we die, ideally, surrendering our suffering and uniting it to the passion of Christ for the good and salvation of all. That is how our suffering is sanctified. That is how we follow Christ on the cross, moving toward Resurrection. Christ's sacrifice has redeemed all mankind, sanctifying all of our suffering and death, for all time. And that is why the heavens rejoice with a God who dances with shouts of joy, for us!

Broken Hallelujah

Morris, an 82 year-old man, went to the doctor to get a physical. A few days later, the doctor saw Morris walking down the street with a gorgeous young woman on his arm. The doctor said, "You're really doing great, aren't you?"

Morris replied, "Just doing what you said, Doc: 'Get a hot mamma and be cheerful.'" The doctor said, "I didn't say that. I said, 'You've got a heart murmur; be careful.'"

Most of us are more careful than Morris when it comes to warnings about our health and future suffering and pain we may encounter. Jesus tells us "You will weep and mourn, but the world will rejoice; you will have pain, but your pain will turn into joy." (John 16:20).

In our world we face some very difficult times, and then we ask, "Why does God allow such terrible things to happen?" Father Brendan McGuire shares some of his reflection at the funeral of a murder suicide that left small children orphaned. "Why would God allow such a horrible thing to happen to such a lovely family?" some ask.

God gives us free will. If God intervened in every situation where we make bad choices God would have to interfere non-stop all over the world, McGuire says. "…these calamities are happening constantly even now. Look at all the people who have been killed in all parts of the world today. 'He [God] would have to intercede in every one of those. And people who are dying of hunger; it is not God's will... It is our wilful ignorance or wilful lack of cooperation with sharing.'"

When it comes to our pain and suffering, we want God to intervene. We will lose the battle for good health and fitness; death is not the end but the beginning. Our moment of death will be the greatest moment of our existence. It will be the time to rejoice in Christ's victory over death.

There is a line in Leonard Cohen's song "Broken Hallelujah" which consoles me in my struggles to be a Christian: "I did my best, it wasn't much … I've told the truth, I didn't come all this way to fool you."

Given our human imperfections, we need to cry out for forgiveness, as Cohen says in his song:

"And even though it all went wrong
I'll stand before the Lord of Song
With nothing on my tongue but Hallelujah."

God loves us so dearly he sacrificed his only son for us. It is only our human nature that makes our attempts at praise sometimes seem like "a cold and very lonely

Hallelujah". God loves us in our brokenness and our loneliness. God is Love.

In this world of pain and suffering, Covid-19 and death, we think about dying and judgement, but we are not afraid. In the front entrance to my home I have a plaque that says *Fürhte dich nicht, denn ich habe dich erlöst!* Which means: Fear not, I have redeemed you. (Isaiah 43:1).

How we choose to think about suffering or hardship is within our control. Believing in the Resurrection enables us to find joy. *The Book of Wisdom* 3:1-9 tells us that the souls of the just are in the hand of God who uses their suffering to refine them like gold in a furnace, then gathers them as a sacrificial offering. The joy of the resurrection follows life's suffering. Taking up our cross daily and living in joy is something we can choose. It beats any of the alternatives.

The Saints teach us about suffering and salvation. Saint Andre of Quebec sowed seeds of hope in the people he met. One of his friends said: "I never brought a sick person to Brother Andre without that person returning home enriched. Some were cured. Others died some time later, but Brother Andre had consoled them."

To live in God's house is heaven. Saint Andre said: "You know, it is permitted to desire death if one's unique goal is to go toward God. When I die, I will go to heaven, I will be much closer to God than I am now; I will have more power to help you."

A few months before his death, those around Saint Andre of Quebec heard him cry out, "I am suffering so much, my God! My God!" And then, in a very weak voice: "Here is the grain," as if referring to the Gospel: "Unless the grain of wheat falls into the ground and dies, it remains alone. But If it dies, it brings forth much fruit." (John 12, 24).

Chapter 14
Gratitude – Living in Love

A real sense of gratitude is lacking in our world. That is one reason many of our churches are not filled on Sunday morning. I am reminded of the story of one worshipper who thanked the minister after the homily and said,

> *"Thanks for the message, Reverend. You must be smarter than Einstein."*
>
> *Beaming with pride, the minister said, "Why, thank you, brother! Exactly what do you mean that I must be smarter than Einstein?"*
>
> *"Well, Reverend, they say that Einstein was so smart that only ten people in the world could understand him. But Reverend, no one can understand you."*

GRATITUDE CAN SAVE YOUR LIFE

In a story of creation the birds at first walked with their little feet, and stumbled and hopped. They complained because they could not walk very fast and they had extra weight on their shoulders, these appendages, and they could not figure out why they were given so much burden.

Then one day, one of the little birds stumbled, and as it stumbled forward, the appendages on its shoulders opened and the wings lifted the bird up into the air. And the bird started to fly. Soon all the birds soared the skies and gave great glory to God because now they could go anywhere at any speed.

We can see our world as a series of connections or a string of coincidences, or we can believe in miracles and celebrate life with a view to eternity. Even during Covid-19 many of us have to admit we are doing just fine. We have jobs, family, friends and a great place to live. We are graced by God with so much. The world has enough mountains and sunrises, enough rainbows and flowers, enough sunsets and stars every day. What we need is more people to appreciate and enjoy it.

Research in psychology and neuroscience tell us that gratitude can be cultivated. We can form habits of gratitude. One way is to list daily five things for which we are grateful.

How does gratitude make you happy? Gratitude is associated with greater happiness. Gratitude helps people feel more positive emotions, relish good experiences, improve their health, deal with adversity, and build strong relationships. "It is impossible to feel grateful and depressed in the same moment." Naomi Williams.

"Give thanks in all circumstances; for this is the will of God in Christ Jesus for you." (1 Thessalonians 5:18). "This is the day that the Lord has made; let us rejoice and be glad in it."(Psalm 118:24). "And let the peace of Christ rule in your hearts, to which indeed you were called in one body. And be thankful." (Colossians 3:15).

The *New York Times*, in a series of three studies, reported that people who wrote five things they were grateful for weekly for two months scored significantly higher on self reported emotional and physical measure. Those people who kept a gratitude journal were more optimistic and felt happier. They reported fewer physical problems and spent more time working out.

In a study of polio survivors and other people with neuromuscular problems, "those who kept a gratitude journal reported feeling happier and more optimistic than those in a control group, and these reports were corroborated by observations from their spouses. These grateful people also fell asleep more quickly at night, slept longer and woke up feeling more refreshed."

In a study of 186 men and women who already had some form of heart disease, researchers found that those who reported a more grateful mindset on a questionnaire were less depressed, slept better, and had more energy. Even more incredible was the fact they exhibited lower levels of both inflammation and plaque build-up. In other words, those participants who were more grateful actually had healthier hearts.

"Memories of past joys help us to grasp onto hope in the midst of darkness, believing that eventually all will be well once more. Joy glories in the love of God and others and effortlessly draws others into that love." (Isabella Moyer).

Geoffrey James of Inc.com says, "People who approach life with a sense of gratitude are constantly aware of what's wonderful in their lives. Because they enjoy the fruits of their successes, they seek out more success. And when things don't go as planned, people who are grateful can put failure into perspective."

Gratitude can save your life through the better health you can enjoy. Gratitude can become a habit, as we see in the gratitude journal studies. Giving thanks can make you happier. Joy can be cultivated.

Harvard Health tells us giving thanks can make us happier. Joy does not need to stop during tough times; in fact, we are better off if we allow a little joy into our struggle. A good way to combat depression, which is hanging around us during this Covid-19 period, is to be in touch with our blessings.

Becky Cane suggests five ways to find joy in tough times: *Use the good dishes, make someone else laugh, throw a party, sing and dance, and wear something joyful.* And Cane suggests, writing down five things you're grateful for is a whole lot easier than getting your butt out the door for a run.

Use some of these advisedly during Covid-19 lockdowns, but we get the point. Gratitude is the key to living with joy. "Gratitude turns what we have into enough, and more. It turns denial into acceptance, chaos into order, confusion into clarity. ... It makes sense of our past, brings peace for today, and creates a vision for tomorrow." *Melody Beattie*

"In life, one has a choice to take one of two paths: to wait for some special day--or to celebrate each special day." *Rasheed Ogunlaru.* We can choose to celebrate the joy of each day. I am reminded of the horse who walks into a bar. The bar tender asks, "Why the long face?"

To be in love is to be grateful

In our family my siblings and I had a little joke to cover any gift that essentially fell short of the mark. "Thank goodness it's the thought that counts," we would say. As children we offered gifts of genuine love, even though we had little to give. A gift certificate for a peanut butter sandwich for example.

As children we anticipated opening a gift on Christmas morning with great expectation. Disappointment sometimes resulted. We echoed the adage "The gift without the giver is bare." To which we added, "The giver without the gift is really bare." As adults we open that gift with a deeper appreciation of the giver.

I will always remember the most heart-warming gift I ever received at Christmas. It was a picture of a dream gift which the giver could not afford to give me. It was indeed the thought that counted. To receive someone's dream as a gift is profound. I am grateful for the imagination and love that inspired that gift. It came from the heart.

The greatest liturgical prayer in the church is the

151

Eucharist, a word that means thanksgiving, or praise, for the wonderful works of God. Just as Jesus raised his eyes to heaven and gave thanks for the bread and wine of the last supper, so we also give thanks to God for the gift of Christ's nourishment of our very souls in the Eucharist. It is our very life, the part of us that is eternal and will never die.

How grateful are we to God for all the gifts of creation we receive with every morning's sunrise? How grateful are we for the first things that come to mind: smiles, humour, variety, love, clouds, rain, dreams, chocolate, spirituality, and grandchildren. On second thought, add music. These will get you through anything.

Gratitude will change our world. One person smiled at me today, and I smiled at the next twenty or so people. If half of these persons smiled at the people they met - you do the Math.

Let me share a great example of the power of gratitude to change a life and the world around it. Nataly Kogan emigrated from Russia at the age of 13. Her early life in America consisted of refugee camps, city housing projects, food stamps, wearing donated clothes and being made fun of endlessly.

To Nataly, surviving the pain of that experience was all about coping, and she focused on becoming happy. Really happy. She decided to follow the American Dream: Achieve a lot of things, be successful, make a lot of money, move on and move up.

Nataly read articles on happiness and followed defined steps to reach her goal. Every day she would write down three good things about her day. She did it every day, even on days when this was a struggle. Her second step was making a rule to say thank you at least once a day. Expressing gratitude to others has been shown to do everything from improving romantic relationships to increasing happiness and decreasing depressive symptoms.

Her third gratitude habit was to pause and savour something once a day. Nataly stopped eating while standing up. She literally stopped to smell the flowers she'd bought for her kitchen. In the end Nataly concluded that practicing gratitude had changed her life. Gratitude is a skill and a habit we can cultivate.

The greatest gratitude we experience on earth is the Eucharistic prayer. The word "Eucharist" is from the Greek word *eucharistia*, which is itself a translation of the Hebrew word *berekah* which means thanksgiving or praise for the wonderful works of God. As we spend time in gratitude with our God, wonderful blessings can occur.

Let me share a personal example. I spent time visiting with Jesus March 24, 2016. It was Holy Thursday, and as we usually do, we had adoration time set aside until midnight, to spend an hour with Jesus and not to fall asleep like the disciples in Gethsemane.

The weather was cooperative. The snow and ice kept many away. So it was that I was relatively alone in church with only a kindred spirit or two respecting our space as Jesus and I visited. I will share some of the thoughts we shared.

My first thoughts were about this book in the very early stages, a book about dying. God thought it would be good to have this around funeral homes to console people who had just lost a loved one. I got excited about how Easter impacts on this particular scene. What consolation and joy on which a grieving family could reflect. Jesus left his followers so that He could send the Spirit and work wonderfully with this new love. After His Resurrection

Jesus could appear to us through closed doors. He could be everywhere we were, and we could better understand the greatest mysteries of His presence.

The Holy Eucharist on this day, Holy Thursday, was a game changer. Every year my mother had us wear our best suits to the celebration on this night when the Mass and the priesthood and the Holy Eucharist were instituted.

As my visit with Jesus continued, we shared about our angels who look after us when we are approaching death, like Jesus in the garden of Gethsemane. And then the messages started coming through to me. As I said, we had a good meeting.

In God's presence our guilt and fears are gone. "I have come so that you may have life and have it more abundantly" John 10:10. The devil tries to steal our lives away, but he is no match for Jesus and the life of Jesus in us. The Eucharist is a game changer.

Easter is the end to all longing, loneliness, angst, wanting – God has kissed us, his creation, and left His mark. His kingdom will come. We will meet face to face with God (I call Jesus God, but that's OK). Then we will thank God for the gifts of children, spouses, friends, family, love, creation!

Thank you, God, for innocence, for all the times Jesus is there for us. Thank you for angels, and for creativity. Thanks for creativity and thousands of ideas; for Art and music. For prayer and visiting with Jesus who strengthens and inspires us and blesses us in countless ways.

Thanks. For letting us touch the hem of Christ's garment and the healing we receive – spiritually and physically. For letting us be Christ to others. For giving us hope that God's Kingdom is coming. For the understanding of mysteries and the Communion of Saints.

For the oneness of being in love in marriage. For Jesus in us. For celibates who experience oneness with God in a special way.

For the efficacy of pain and suffering which redeem us and in turn help us redeem others. For sickness and wasting away in terminal illness which makes us ready to leave this wonderful earth.

Easter lifts us from the despair of death. Our death is our Easter experience, our remaking into new life where darkness is replaced by light, by the Light of Christ. Let the angel of God roll back the big stone in our lives so that we can see the empty tomb where our despair used to dwell.

As I left that one-hour Holy Thursday visit with God I was reminded of a poet's perception of God and eternity:

"To see a World in a Grain of Sand
And a Heaven in a Wild Flower,
Hold Infinity in the palm of your hand
And Eternity in an hour." -William Blake.

Sometimes suffering, pain or life's traumas distract us from the true joy of a Christian. Let me share the example of Maya Anderson, poet. At eight, due to some trauma, she stopped speaking. A lady in town, over lemonade, read poetry to Maya and explained that poetry was music written for the human voice. She encouraged Maya to read. She did, at first hidden under her mother's bed, and then in the open. Later she began to write and recite. Her true voice returned.

The coming of death in our lives is a game changer but it cannot take us from our set course and our faith in

155

Jesus. I cannot imagine Mary, the Mother of Jesus, being anything but full of Grace even on the day they were crucifying Christ. And Jesus, on the cross, was still filled with his mission of salvation when he said to Dismas, "This day you will be with me in paradise."

When someone we love is dying, when we get a dreadful diagnosis, then we find our perspective of reality challenged.

Someone observed recently that the church does not do a good job of helping us handle suffering and pain. These are tough areas to accommodate. But Jesus helps us through the Cross, and that is the universal sign in any church. It points to another world, another reality.

Wake up lovers; it is time to start the
journey! We've seen enough of this world; it is
time to see another. -Rumi

The Persian poet Rumi gives us a challenging wake up call for that time in our lives when we ponder the great mystery that our physical decay is also the beginning of life.

Joy and hope are not lost when our physical strength and beauty wane. We are reminded of a loving God in the words of a song echoing Jeremiah 31: "I have loved you with an everlasting love. I have called you, and you are mine."

Every day is still a gift from a loving God. True, it brings us one day closer to that union with love and all the saints. Now is that a cause for worry?

Time is a great mystery. Time can heal. Time can seem endless, and it can seem fleeting. However we experience it, we know that God is outside of time.

156

Whether we now measure time by the hour, by the day or by the year, God is with us, pouring out grace and comfort.

"Be still and know that I am God." (Psalm 46:10).

Before we leave this chapter on Gratitude I want to share an experience I recently had that puts a perspective on gratitude and the last chapter of life. In 2019 my wife and I celebrated our fiftieth wedding anniversary. Part of the program included a slide tape of our story.

Usually you see this type of life review at a funeral, but it is amazing to see many milestones of your life and family celebrated like that. It was profound in its impact. And I was left with a deep gratitude.

I was diagnosed with cancer ten years ago, and I sometimes found myself standing in the doorway looking at my family celebrating a meal, wondering if this is what it would look like without me. I realized that the past ten years were all blessing. Marriages of my children and nine grandchildren were some of the highlights. And the love! There is an immeasurable amount of love blessings that just keep coming.

It does not have to be a momentous event in your life like a fiftieth Anniversary to touch gratitude. Recently as I watched a travel agent's commercial about visiting a paradise island, I thought of the paradise we take for granted every day. Immigrants dream of a place like this and risk their lives and the lives of their families to get here.

And many of us here take for granted so much we have to be thankful for. A litany of gratitude spontaneously breaks forth:

Today I had enough to eat. / Thank you God.
Today I was warm. / Thank you God.
Today I saw the sun shine and heard the wind blow. / Thank you God.
Today I smelled a rose. / Thank you God.
Today I whistled. / Thank you God.
Today I slept deeply. / Thank you God.
Today I had no pain. / Thank you God.
Today I could run. / Thank you God.
Today I had clear thoughts. / Thank you God.
Today I laughed. / Thank you God.
Today I could pray. / Thank you God.
Today I prayed for dearly departed. / Thank you God.
Today I dreamed about the future. / Thank you God.
Today I loved. / Thank you God.
Today I felt someone else's sadness. / Thank you God.
Today I could sing. / Thank you God.
Today I forgave someone. / Thank you God.
Today I felt peace. / Thank you God.
Today I took deep breaths. / Thank you God.
Today I rested. / Thank you God.

We do not earn these blessings, but God gives them to us out of love. In Psalm 65 King David gives thanks to God:

Praise awaits you, our God, in Zion;
to you our vows will be fulfilled.
You who answer prayer,
to you all people will come.
When we were overwhelmed by sins,
you forgave our transgressions.
Blessed are those you choose
and bring near to live in your courts!
We are filled with the good things of your
house,
of your holy temple.
...

The whole earth is filled with awe at your
wonders;
where morning dawns, where evening fades,
you call forth songs of joy.
You care for the land and water it;
you enrich it abundantly. ...
you soften it with showers and bless its
crops.
You crown the year with your bounty,
and your carts overflow with abundance.
The grasslands of the wilderness overflow;
the hills are clothed with gladness.
The meadows are covered with flocks
and the valleys are mantled with grain;
they shout for joy and sing.

The God who loves us really loves us! As I continue on the road all runners come, I have a light heart. I invite the reader to the final chapter, *Heaven Bound Amid Pandemics*.

Chapter 15
The Road All Runners Come

When it comes time to die, be not like those
whose hearts are
filled with the fear of death, so when their
time comes they
weep and pray for a little more time to live
their lives over
again in a different way. Sing your death
song, and die
like a hero going home.
- Mohican Chief Aupumut, 1725

A Paraguayan pilot, Gus Encina, was traveling on the flight carrying the Brazilian soccer team of Chapecoense in Medellín (Colombia) that ended in tragedy November 11, 2016.

Gus died in the crash. Encina posted this message on social media just before the crash: "Where do you look for your life? Forward or behind? May the Lord grant you the grace to leave things behind, even those which you consider precious in this life, and may he allow you to look ahead, where Christ is waiting for you, for a glorious meeting that will open the gates of eternity."

Joy in the Afterlife

Hy Goldfarb was to be knighted for his many generous works. Not knowing any Latin, he decided to say something in Hebrew when knighted. He would repeat the question the son asks the father on the first night of Passover.

As he knelt before the Queen, she placed her sword on one shoulder and then the other, and motioned for Hy to speak.

Out came, "Ma nishtana ha leila hazeh."

The queen turned to her husband Prince Philip and said, "Why is this knight different from all the other knights?"

Why is the death of a Christian different from other deaths? We all know of people who have lived a happy life and been blessed with death at its conclusion. Michael Gartner, once President of NBC News, tells a story about his father.

In his nineties Michael's father said you have a choice: you can walk through life and enjoy it, or you can drive through life and miss it. At this point his wife interjected with, "He hit a horse."

"Well," my [Michael's] father said, "there was that, too."

Michael relates the event of his father's death at 102

years. One night his father said, "You know, I'm probably not going to live much longer." That night his son and daughter sat up with him through the night. At one point, noticing the gloomy looks on his children's faces he said, "I would like to make an announcement. No one in this room is dead yet."

An hour or so later, he spoke his last words: "I want you to know," he said, clearly and lucidly, "that I am in no pain. I am very comfortable. And I have had as happy a life as anyone on this earth could ever have." A short time later, he died.

An African proverb says: the death of an old man [or woman] is like the burning of a library. There is a treasure-trove of experience and wisdom in a long life – a library full. And when the library is gone, no matter how strong our faith or how strong our belief in eternal life, we have every right to be sad.

My sister tells the story about her husband who had died some years ago. Her daughter was cooking soup in a pressure cooker when it exploded. There was hot soup all over the room except for the small space where the baby sat in her chair. Some time later, when the little baby had grown and was able to talk, someone was showing her a picture of her Grandfather. She babbled excitedly, "I know him. He protected me from the soup."

Our loved ones surely offer consolation and strength to us even after they are gone. And the church, at the time of death, is there to offer assurance to those who grieve; assurance that life continues after death. And so, in faith, we continue to trust in the great love of Jesus our Redeemer who has promised to prepare a place for those who are his followers.

Levity, and stories that console and inspire? And yet

facing our mortality leaves us uneasy, to say the least. Let me try one more inspiration.

Imagine a strong, healthy, charismatic leader in your family circle. Also imagine this person to be gifted and talented beyond reason. He can walk on water. He is perfect in every way. He is loving, forgiving, insightful, perceptive and a gifted communicator. His stories are famous. Now imagine this person will be taken from you by death. If you are like me, you do not have to imagine hard because someone we love is dying right now. Though he or she is not like Christ in every way, he or she is sharing in the suffering of Christ, which opened a door out of this imperfect world.

"The whole of creation is eagerly waiting for God to reveal his sons." (Romans 8:19). Creation is enslaved by man's fall but still retains the hope of being freed. Our bodies are stuck in this imperfect world and our suffering and groaning are a sign that we wait for deliverance.

"You are sad now, but I shall see you again, and your hearts will be full of joy, and that joy no one shall take from you." (John 16:22).

Now think of your loved one who is dying or has died. He or she has gone into that joy promised by Jesus. Would you deny him that reward after his earthly trials and suffering? Having finished the race, her journey, would you deny her the crown and bring her back again, like Lazarus who had to die again?

Jesus left us so that the Holy Spirit could come to enlighten us, give us strength and guide our journey. With the help of that Spirit we can realise the eternal truths that bring us consolation even in this sometime vale of tears.

"If we live, we live for the Lord; and if we die, we die for the Lord, so that alive or dead, we belong to the

Lord." (Romans 14:7-9). Great minds through the ages have puzzled about the mystery of our "leaving" this world. Now, thanks be to Jesus, we can live our lives with absolute truths.

"We want you to be quite certain, brothers, about those who have died, to make sure you do not grieve about them, like people who have no hope. We believe Jesus died and rose again, and that it will be the same for those who have died in Jesus …. We shall stay with the Lord forever. With such thoughts as these you should comfort one another." (1 Thessalonians 4:13-18).

Even with all the "knowledge of the head" we may still need to set our hearts free. Grief at the loss of someone we love dearly is a process we cannot skip. We can, however, lift our hands to God, lift our burdens and let them go. Put the sorrow we cannot handle into God's hands. Then we can find peace.

In Eugene O'Neill's play *Beyond the Horizon*, a character speaks of death:

> You mustn't feel sorry for me. Don't you see I'm happy at last — free — free! — freed from the farm — free to wander on and on — eternally! Look! Isn't it beautiful beyond the hills? I can hear the old voices calling me to come — And this time I'm going! It isn't the end. It's a free beginning — the start of my voyage! I've won to my trip — the right of release — beyond the horizon! Oh, you ought to be glad — glad — for my sake!
>
> (Robert: Act 3, Scene 2)

Truly, when our time comes, we can look to *the hills beyond*. In Thomas Wolfe's *Don't you know you can't go home again* the title is reinforced in the denouement of the novel in which Webber realises: "You can't go back home to your family, back home to your childhood ... back home to a young man's dreams of glory and of fame ... back home to places in the country, back home to the old forms and systems of things which once seemed everlasting but which are changing all the time – back home to the escapes of Time and Memory."

The time will come when we can no longer return to the narrow confines of our previous way of life and then our youthful memories will fail. Like Christ, we are born to be Kings, but as nature runs its course, we are reduced to nothingness as we die. That is the paradox of suffering – it is debilitating as it limits and defines us physically. But united with Christ it expands to eternal and grand dimensions as we join the Saints in heaven.

So it is with our significant achievements. Like our dreams of fame, they fade in this place "where glory does not stay". "Naked I came from my mother's womb, naked I shall return." (Job 1:21). Then all is left in the hands of God.

In Chapter 13 on Pain and Suffering we saw St Andre of Quebec cry out, "I am suffering so much, my God! My God!" And then, in a very weak voice, offering his death to God: "Here is the grain … if it dies, it brings forth much fruit." (John 12, 24).

As death approaches us who do we call? As Christ hung on the cross he turned to Mary and said, "Woman, this is your son." And turning to John, the disciple he loved, Jesus said, "This is your mother." As followers of

Christ we call Mary our Mother. And in all the Hail Marys we recite during our lives we pray, "Pray for us sinners now and at the hour of our death". Mary is our Mother we turn to in life and especially at the hour of our deaths.

Let us live free of the fear of death! How? Let me share a story Father Gerard Dowling tells. Dowling points out how Catholics who grew up in the church can so easily turn to Mary when they need help. Hail Marys trip off their tongues easily.

Dowling says it all started at his mother's knee. She passed on the devotion to Mary to him and his siblings. As a family they prayed the Rosary every night. Seeing their mother and dad kneel as they prayed, encouraged turning to Mary and Jesus for help.

His sister Mary joined Father Dowling daily at St Cecilia's Church for the Rosary the last thirteen years of Mary's life. Dowling visited Mary in the nursing home as she was dying. Praying the Rosary continued to be a great comfort after Mary died. Mary had gone on to the place Jesus prepared for her.

Trusting in our Mother Mary and praying for her daily intercession, "Pray for us sinners now and at the hour of our death", allows us to live worry free. We can trust in a loving Mother and Son, our Brother Jesus, who care for us and guide our every step.

A Moment with Mary – Daily Reflection says:

> The hour of the Passion of Jesus is also
> the hour of the compassion of the Virgin.
> Pray for that hour so that it is the hour of
> Mary, Consoler of the Afflicted as well!

Common experience shows that many of the dying spontaneously call for Mother Mary.

If we pray to Mary at the hour of our death it is also because she alone, since the day of her Assumption, joined her Son Jesus in the glory of heaven with her body and her soul. So figuratively speaking, she can greet us in Paradise like a "good hostess." This is why the liturgy of the Church calls her the "gate always open to heaven" and beseeches us to look at the star to reach the port of heaven.

Going Home

As a well-spent day brings happy sleep,
so a life well spent brings happy death.
- Leonardo da Vinci

In all the world there is no better feeling than coming home. There is no stronger word to capture the emotions: home for Christmas, home for the holidays, homeward bound. Remember the fondest home comings! One Christmas Eve my brother came home in the late afternoon, in a bit of a prairie storm, to fill our hearts that were worried he would be unable to join us.

My granddaughter came running through security at the airport. "I'm going to give them such a big hug," she said. Three hours of delicious visiting as we drove home through the night.

Poets and song writers have expressed it so aptly:

167

Home is the sailor, home from sea.
And the hunter home from the hill.
("Requiem" Robert Louis Stevenson)

In Homer's epic tale *The odyssey* Ulysses spends ten years trying to return home to his wife and son and his beloved homeland Ithaca. There is nothing sweeter in all the world than coming home.

As pilgrims from another world we are all journeying towards our eternal home. One hymn puts it best:

Going home, going home
I'm just going home…
It's not far, just close by
Through an open door.

At the end of a long life we expect the sweet reward of home:

Momma's there expecting me
Papa's waiting, too
Lots of folk gathered there
All the friends I knew.

To that place where there are no tears, no pain:

Nothing's lost, all's gain
No more fret nor pain…
Wide awake with a smile
Going on and on.

I look at the farmhouse where my siblings and I grew up with Mom and Dad. The house is empty now. No longer do we gather there as family and know *home*. Like pilgrims seeking another home we make the emotional adjustments.

My grandfather's house no longer stands on the prairie. But it is more than dust in the wind. All who once lived there have gone home "through that open door". And there is much to celebrate! In time all our siblings and we will join the generations that have gone before us.

Love is the constant! When we depart this realm, we take love with us. To people of faith there is much to celebrate. Life begins on this earth, but it does not end here:

> *Momma's there expecting me*
> *Papa's waiting, too*
> *Lots of folk gathered there.*
> (Lyrics by William Arms Fisher
> Music by Dvorak))

When *our work is all done, our cares laid by,* like it says in "Going Home", we will have no more fears. *"Our real life begun"*, we will be *"wide awake with a smile"*. There is much to be thankful for.

Ray of Light

"They [our mothers] give birth astride a grave, the light gleams an instant, then it's night once more." (from Samuel Beckett's *Waiting for Godot*).

Our lives are so much more than a flash of light. Our mothers and fathers give us more than birth astride a grave. For most of us a family unit surrounds us and even nurtures us physically and spiritually. The church provides a meaningful experience of the gleam of light and helps ward off the threat of the darkness of death and sin. Surely our lives are more significant than such a brief moment - birth astride a grave - devoid of deeper purpose. We have a choice. We can make our lives more meaningful than that.

Another line follows in the next speech of Becket's play: "We have time to grow old. The air is full of our cries." While you and I have time in this world, we can do more than fill the air with our cries.

We can work in the vineyard. For too significant numbers of us the real conversion never takes hold. The grain sprouts on the path and then shrivels. At one point in our lives we stood up or our godparents stood up for us and professed, "This is our Faith! This is what we believe! This is what we commit our lives to!" Then we got caught up in the humdrum of daily life and lived in a state of doubt and non-commitment. The actions of our lives reflect whether we are children of God.

How do we live lives that are reflective of our enlightenment as God's children? How do we shine out in a world that is often dark?

The resurrection light of Christ blazes forth in a world that is too often dark. Dostoevsky, once arrested and sentenced to death for treason, describes the experience of how "He was taken to a square in St. Petersburg and read the death sentence. He watched as soldiers aimed rifles at his comrades. Just then a pardon arrived. Dostoevsky later wrote his brother: "Life is a gift; life is happiness …. If youth only knew!"

Imagine the tremendous release, the great freedom experienced in this deliverance. But imagine the greater liberation of those who were offered no reprieve but were gathered into the arms of a loving Father in a place where there are no more fears, no more tears, no hunger, no injustice; where they truly are with the Risen Christ. They joined Christ on the cross and now enjoy the promise made to Dismas: "Today you will be with me in paradise."

And so Christ's love still blazes through the dark. The love of our brothers and sisters, some of whom have gone home before us, binds us in the family of God and keeps us from the darkness of death. The light of all the pain and suffering, our own included, offered as prayer, redeems us and illumines our final hour.

Light is still the best metaphor to describe Christ's life in us. Every night we fall asleep into physical darkness, so like to death. We struggle for ways to express the light we seek in our dark world.

Every night the air covers itself with blood
and on awakening everything returns as before
The icy wind is following our existence
and we talk about strange dreams
(from "Fourth ray of light" – Kirlian Camera)

In looking for a muse, a song whose music would sustain me through the months it would take to give birth to this book, I found my inspiration in Madonna's "Ray of Light", about which one internet critic says: "Madonna feels like she just got home because she is the Ray of Light she's singing, writing and crying about – all done with a smile and tears to balance it out." The critic goes on to say,

"Madonna believes in Love because she is Home. 'Ray of Light' then is about the wonderment – the Joy and Sadness, Happiness and Sorrow of her life."

Madonna's version of "Ray of Light" begins with Zephyr in the night sky echoing the theme from "Fourth ray of light" where light dies in the red glow of sunset, but life begins anew at dawn, and "we talk about strange dreams" like the Judeo-Christian Resurrection stories. Indeed the "faster than the speeding light" of Madonna's song conjures images of resurrection beyond the physical and at the least hints at "home" in the sense of heaven bound.

Our life's journey is going home to the Father. From the moment of our conception we move forward by degrees until our journey ends at natural death. Sorry, there is no softening that reality. Or is there? Life can be filled with joy and hope, not to mention love, which all combined make this a wonderful trip. We can choose to live a life sparkling with joy and hope or we can entertain sadness and sin. The realization of God's daily presence makes all the difference. Faith is what makes it all possible. And the greatest life is one that enjoys God's daily presence.

In the planning stages of this book I was struck by the fact that my mother was born 100 years ago. She was called to eternal life at fifty-eight, and I muse that the last forty-two years must have seemed like heaven to her. I'm sure she still feels like she just got home.

And so, dear reader, I leave us with the challenge to choose a life of hope in the light of the Resurrection. Our lives are laid down in service to family, spouse, friends, community and world. There is no fear of death, but only gratitude for life.

Finally, God gathers us all in tender hands, loving and forgiving.

> "Death is not the extinguishing of light,
> but putting out the lamp so the dawn may
> come." -India Mystic

Acknowledgments

Thanks to *The Word Among Us* for many inspirations and the occasional short quote.

Thanks for inspirations from *Dynamic Christian, A Moment with Mary* and *Spirit Daily*.

Thanks also to:
Angels on Earth Magazine
Roses in December by Marilyn Heavilin
Proof of Heaven by Eben Alexander M.D.
Spirituality for Dummies by Sharon Janis
Sacred Heart, Gateway to God by Wendy M. Heart
And special thank you to Father Mark Miller for his workshop on *Proper Care of the Dying* - Palliative Care and Euthanasia;
to Dr. Bill Webster for *Healing Strategies after a loss,* and to Father Ron Rolheiser for much support and sharing thoughts on Suicide and Spirituality in general.